To Bou

Alan & Cindy

Enjoy the Read

Lotus of Kashmir

Bob Saunders

PEN NAME OF AUBREY

ISBN: 978-1-914933-25-7

Bob Saunders

Copyright 2022

All rights reserved. No part of this publication may be reproduced, stored in a retrieval system or transmitted in any form or by any means, electronic, mechanical, photocopy, recording or otherwise, without prior written consent of the copyright owner. Nor can it be circulated in any form of binding or cover other than that in which it is published and without similar condition including this condition being imposed on a subsequent purchaser.

The right of Bob Saunders to be identified as the author of this work has been asserted in accordance with the Copyright Designs and Patents Act 1988.

A copy of this book is deposited with the British Library.

Published By: -

i2i
PUBLISHING

i2i Publishing. Manchester.
www.i2ipublishing.co.uk

Chapter 1
Destination Kashmir

Wednesday 30th July 1947. It is just about two weeks to the Partition of the huge sub-continent of India and the worsening situation of religious mania and turmoil. Ken and I are ready at 09.30 hours for five days' leave in Kashmir. We will not be deterred on our plan to visit that province of India in the Himalayas. We are both National Service men. In my case, I joined the RAF at eighteen years old in 1945 with no girlfriend yet. Ken is three years older than me, but his call-up was deferred for three years to allow him to complete his course of toolmaking before joining up. He has a steady girlfriend and they intend to get engaged on his return from overseas. We make our way down to the main entrance of the camp and the bus is waiting for us on the main road near to the Guardroom and close to the Camp MT (Motor Transport).

We are on a temporary posting to a Hill Station called Lower Topa in the foothills of the Himalayas near a town named Murree. During the summer months, all British forces normally have a 'cooling-off period' for three weeks from the extreme heat of the Indian Plains. But because it is only about a fortnight to the Partition of the vast sub-continent, we are stranded up here and unable to travel back to our main camp because rioting is occurring, with trains being stopped, and it would be too dangerous to travel. Up to now, we have been at the Hill Station for nine days and we were told that our return to Lahore will be delayed for a few weeks. This has given us the great opportunity to book five days and four nights in Srinagar, the capital of Kashmir, in the 'real' Himalayas and only 150 miles from this camp.

Immediately on seeing our public transport and anticipating the journey ahead of us, I nicknamed it 'the coffin on wheels'. Ahead of us, we have to traverse a rugged, harsh and beautiful mountain road stretching for the 150 miles from Lower Topa all the way to Srinagar. The route is among the Pir Panjal range of mountains, part of the mighty Himalayas, and we are stopping at a bridge called Saligram. We will be going through a range of mountains with peaks averaging a height of 15,000 feet, with the road weaving its way along a tortuous road. It will mainly be only a single lane with passing places occasionally. Drivers on these roads must need to be telepathic to know when to meet oncoming traffic at passing places.

But first, the bus has to take us downhill from the Guardroom at 6800 feet above sea level to Kohala down at 1938 feet, a big drop in twenty-five miles. This is the border between the Punjab and Kashmir. Nearing Kohala, the River Jhelum appears ahead.

Our bus near Camp.

Border control at Kohala, on the far bank is Kashmir.

Just a very short section of the 'untamed' road.

From camp, the journey down took no more than an hour for the twenty-five miles to the border crossing into Kashmir. This western part of Kashmir would become the new part of the new country of Pakistan and would be known after Partition as Azad Kashmir, stretching from the border town of Kohala to approximately halfway to Srinagar. But at this time, when Ken and I are travelling here, it is still the Punjab in India. Soon after, we stop briefly at the Police Halt for all passengers to pay the toll fee.

We continue the short way to reach Kohala Bridge. A crossing was constructed here in 1877 but disappeared during a flood in 1890. A new steel bridge was erected in 1899. This was my gateway into Kashmir in 1947, but that bridge, in turn, was washed away in 1990. It is reported that a third bridge was built, seemingly at a different spot. We turned right onto the bridge, leaving the Punjab behind us, and alighted in Kashmir. At the end of the bridge was the Kashmiri Custom House, where we stayed for a short while in the heat of the 'plains'. There is a village of Kohala, but not on the main road, so I never spotted it when we passed through the area, not even a glimpse in passing. Precisely at midday, we set off again and still had 125 miles of rough travel to reach our destination. But I can say that we had now truly arrived in Kashmir.

As we entered Kashmir, I recalled an article that went something like this; it captures its attraction very well:

"Kashmir has attractions for all tastes and hobbies, for the lover of sport, hunting, swimming and boating, for the tourist no less than for the geologist, botanist and archaeologist. But it is, par excellence, the land for trekking and mountaineering. And though its varied charms last the year round, it is during the summer months (May to October) that the call of Kashmir becomes irresistible. Outside Kashmir – the grey aridity of the plains shimmering in the summer sun, grey leafless trees few and far between, providing just enough shade for the lurking cobra or viper, hot debilitating winds blowing restlessness far into the night – blinding dust storms are welcome, as anything is welcome which may break up the sultry monotony of those dog days. The day begins and ends in the morning. They may come to life again for a short while in the evening till mosquitoes, moths, gnats and wasps send one to bed and the shelter of its mosquito nets. We get up to greet the hot glare of the sun and must rise with the lark and the only sight to cool us is the sight or thought of the distant snow-capped heights of Kashmir, which the memory of other days will bring to our mind. Then the lure of Kashmir, its hills and lakes and flowers with their nostalgic fascination, becomes irresistible indeed."

From the border bridge at Kohala, we set off in a northerly direction and basically followed the left bank of the River Jhelum towards the city of Muzaffarabad, aiming for the area where a tributary of the River Jhelum joins at the bridge at Domel. We had hardly travelled more than six miles past Kohala when we stopped for tiffin (lunch) by the side of the river at this small village called Domel in Kashmir.

Chapter 2
The End and the Beginning. And how did I get to India?

While we were having lunch at the remote village of Domel, I reflected on how I got here. Ending up over 7000 miles from home and never having been away on my own before.

8th May 1945 (VE Day) – the end of the war in Europe. Just over two months later, on the 19th of July, I would be 18 years old and at the age to begin National Service. Coincidentally, my father was born in 1900 and reached 18 years of age in the year that the First World War ended. Quite a coincidence for both of us to be of age when the two world wars ended in the twentieth century. There was no conscription after the First World War, but after the Second World War, conscription carried on for at least ten years. Mothers all over the world worry about their children, so I told mine, "Don't worry, Ma. Now that it is all over in Europe, they won't need me."

14th August (VJ Day, Victory in Japan Day) – precisely the day I received my 'Calling Up' papers for National Service. Of course, now that the dreadful world war was over, I was sure that I would not be needed – "Don't worry Ma, this is just a formality." But not long after, there was a letter in the post asking me to make a choice between the Army, Navy, Air Force or coal mines. I chose the Air Force, not expecting to be assigned to my chosen branch of the Armed Forces, because I had heard that no-one was accepted for their original choice. In a short while, I heard that I was to report to Padgate, on the edge of Warrington, then in Lancashire, for National Service in the… Royal Air Force! But even now I said, "Don't worry Ma. I will be out within a week and on my way home."

I duly reported to Padgate and they proceeded to issue me with my Air Force kit. I was given a special, peculiar, unusual and unique haircut and went through the comic ritual of the Medical. I will disregard any more reference to that, as it has been done to death. If you don't know, ask an ex-serviceman! Every sprog was allocated two numbers upon joining. First, your Service number, and on Pay Parades when your name was called, you marched up smartly to the desk and stated clearly, "Sir" and your surname and last three numbers of your Service number. Then you received your pay. The second number was your Demobilisation (Demob) number. More about that number later, much later… a long way to go. Now, I realised that I was a member of the illustrious RAF and as the Second World War ends, my National Service begins.

One week later, I was leaving Padgate, not on my way home, but en route to a camp at a place called Deenethorpe, out in the 'wilds' of Northamptonshire, a few miles from the town of Corby. This was a town in an area rich in iron ore and became known for iron and steel departments. We lads knew that we were near our camp when we passed the blast furnace on the outskirts of the town, a tall chimney belching out, not smoke, but pure flames many feet into the air. As we walked into camp for the first time, a very popular song by Bing Crosby was playing, called 'Don't Fence Me In'. No comment! Also popular at the time was a wartime song with appropriate words for my situation, and for many others too. It was called 'Ma, I Miss your Apple Pie', composed jointly by John Jacob Loeb and Carmen Lombardo. The main singer was also Carmen Lombardo, and contrary to his first name, he was the younger brother of Guy Lombardo, a famous band leader.

Deenethorpe is where we received our basic military training, known famously as 'Square Bashing'. In our large hut, there were many sprogs like me, such as Norman from Bentley in Doncaster, Yorkshire; D.R. from Carshalton, Surrey; Les from Tonbridge in Kent; A.R.J. from Tottenham, London; Fred from Willenhall,

Staffs; A.G. from Kenilworth, Warwickshire; Gordon from Bolsover, Derbyshire; Gerald from Watford, Hertfordshire; D.J. from London, SE5; Claude from Sutton Valence, near Maidstone, Kent; Doug from Norwich; Alan from Bristol and Roy from Bridgwater in Somerset. We were a 'mixed bag' from all over England. The normal (if you could call it normal) routines were varied and many. One of the delights was the renowned kit inspection, not only to show your uniform, bedding and equipment, but it all had to be displayed in a certain way. For example, your blanket had to be folded in a particular way and to a precise shape and size. And all the other articles had to be placed around in the correct position. In other words, all the bedsides had to be uniform. Perhaps that is where the word 'uniform' came from. Totally connected to the kit inspection is the polishing. Your boots and the brass buttons on your tunic demanded to see the reflection of your face in them. Boot polish you had to buy; but issued to you is the button stick. It is a metal strip with a slot down lengthways. The button is placed in the slot before polishing and then protects the cloth from being damaged by the polish. Ingenious! Another daily repetitive routine is the Roll Call and other parades, the best one of course being the Pay Parade.

Time heals, so I cannot recall much of the bad stuff and can remember more of the good and funny things. Apart from the drill that was 'drilled' into us, we also had weapon training. The sprogs were issued with rifles, while the officers received pistols. We had to also tackle the stripping and cleaning of our issued rifles. To clean the barrel (very important) we were supplied with a small square of cloth to pull through the barrel. This piece of cloth, believe it or not, was called a 'pull through'. I found that rifles gave a bad kick if not held correctly and I took more to the Sten gun (which I heard was invented to use up an unusual size of bullets, captured in the North African campaign against

Rommel). Our corporal was a master with the Sten gun, while demonstrating how to use it, he made a tin can dance at 50 paces! We learnt how to use the guns while wearing gas masks, and the art of throwing hand grenades. One time, practising on these, I remember a grenade, instead of going way past our barrier, travelled almost straight up and landed just over the barrier. Luckily, it failed to go off. Our unhappy corporal in charge had to go out to retrieve it!

Another time, we were divided into two groups, the first had to go around the countryside spreading pieces of paper and the second group followed them around picking them up! We all thought it was very odd at the time, but it was probably a 'lesson in discipline'.

One weekend, I felt a bit homesick, and because other lads were slipping out of camp without weekend passes, I decided to go too. All went well until about lunchtime on the Sunday. I just happened to look out of our front window at home and to my surprise and horror, I noticed an RAF sergeant standing at a corner almost opposite. I spent a very uncomfortable few minutes (it seemed like hours) checking regularly to see if he was still there. He was. Eventually, I noticed a young woman come to meet him and off they went together on a date. I was relieved to say the least. I thought he was waiting to pounce when I came out to return to camp.

On one leave, I went to London and a highlight was my visit to the Stage Door Canteen. The first was opened in 1942, in the Broadway theatre district of New York. And by November 1945, they were operating in eight US cities, also London and Paris. They catered for all Allied forces, offering food and non-alcoholic drinks, dancing and entertainment, all free. At its peak, it welcomed 10,000 Allied forces on seven nights a week. It was their opportunity to socialise with celebrities, no matter how famous. A remarkable place, which I believe was situated in

Piccadilly. Stars of stage, screen and radio appeared there, no matter how famous. Probably one of the most legendary to appear was Julia Elizabeth Wells. Never heard of her! She wasn't so well known when she appeared at eleven years old on 5th December 1946 at the London Stage Door Canteen. She was named after her grandmothers, Julia Morris and Elizabeth Wells. Her father, Edward C. Wells, was a teacher and her mother Barbara, a pianist and piano teacher. Unfortunately, they divorced when Julia was only four. Later on, her mother married a vaudeville entertainer and Julia joined them in a family stage act, even performing together in the Birmingham parks. Her stepfather's name was Ted Andrews. Julia changed her name to Julie, and so Julie Andrews was born – or reborn!

I was unlucky not to see any of the big stars on my visit to the Stage Door Canteen, but I was very impressed particularly with one attraction there. In the foyer, I believe, was situated a continually running fountain, not chocolate, but of one of the famous names in cola. Just collect a glass and fill it whenever you want. I still like the drink to this day. An American sailor at the time coined the phrase about the Stage Door Canteen, "No liquor, but damned good anyway." If it was good enough for him, it was good enough for me! Though the Canteen was free of charge for food, drink and entertainment, the money had to come from somewhere. New Yorkers responded generously. In fact, all rallied round. Even Irving Berlin contributed by writing a song and donating all the profits. The title was 'I left my heart at the Stage Door Canteen', which became quite popular.

An 'offshoot' of the Stage Door was the Hollywood Canteen. Actor John Garfield (noted for gangster roles) and Bette Davis (needs no introduction) were the driving force behind the project. In 1944, there was a movie entitled *Hollywood Canteen* to advertise it, also to partly promote Hollywood itself. It starred Joan Leslie, Robert Hutton and Dane Clark, but the film was more noted for the appearance of numerous movie stars in cameo roles. To name just a few: Jack Benny, Joe E. Brown, Eddie Cantor, Joan Crawford, Sydney Greenstreet, Paul Henreid, Ida Lupino, Peter Lorre, Eleanor Parker, Roy Rogers (including Trigger, his horse!), S.Z. Sakall, Barbara Stanwyck, Jane Wyman and Jimmy Dorsey and his orchestra. Quite a cast! By the end of 1946, all the Canteens had closed, but lived on in the memories of millions of the Allied forces of World War II.

About this time, November 1945, the eyes of the world turned to a place in Germany, Nuremberg, for the series of trials of Nazi war criminals, arising out of the Second World War. The tribunals lasted until 1949 and it was appropriate that they should be held at Nuremberg, as it was the stage for the Nazi Rallies prior to the war.

The weeks passed slowly, but eventually it was time to move on to our next camp for trade training. In our hut, there was an extensive medley of trades. Mine was to be (after tests) an 'Equipment Assistant' and my time would be to supply – er – equipment, of course! But there were many other trades. Other lads were going to be in Motor Transport or the Military Police, or train as medical orderlies, clerks, cooks or fabric workers. Yes, numerous trades helped to keep the aeroplanes flying. All this trade training was to be at a camp near Blackpool, at a place called Kirkham. Up to 1945, thousands were trained there, not just from Britain and the Commonwealth, but from many other parts of the world as well. I don't remember much about the camp or the training. But one thing I recall is servicemen (and women) doing well with hitch-hiking, so I decided to try it. Now whether it was because the war had finished or I was just useless at it, I failed miserably. For the nine miles to Blackpool, I had about four or five separate lifts to get there, and I cannot even remember how I got back to the camp at Kirkham! In the swinging sixties, part of it was fated to become an open prison.

As the trade training came to an end, we all received our postings. Most of the lads were scheduled for overseas. I was allocated India on draft number 1588, but we all felt sorry for poor Les--- he was assigned not just to Borneo, but to a remote island just off the northern coast called Labuan, reputed to be 'headhunter country'! My posting was very civilised compared to that.

But first, we were all posted to Essex at a place called North Weald in the Epping Forest. This fighter base was founded in 1916 during World War One and played an important role in the Battle of Britain. There was a rumour that Group Captain Sir Douglas Bader was stationed there at the time, but with thousands of service personnel on camp, I certainly never met him. I would have liked to have seen him, for he was a legend in his own lifetime. He lost both legs in a flying accident before the Second World War, but that never stopped him from being a famous and successful fighter pilot during the Battle of Britain. Eventually, he was shot down over Europe in August 1941 and was taken captive. The German troops were amazed that he had no legs! He was liberated by the Allied troops in April 1945, after a sojourn at Colditz Castle. Back in Britain, his return to action was denied. However, he led the victory fly-past of 300 planes over London at the end of the war and left the RAF finally in February 1946. His remarkable story was told in a 1956 film, *Reach for the Sky,* starring Kenneth More, which won a BAFTA film award.

For me, it was now nearing the end of January 1946 when I arrived at North Weald, just overlapping with Group Captain Bader by about a month. But even if I had met him, I doubt if he would have spoken to me, just a lowly AC2 (Aircraftman Second Class) – the rank given when you first join up.

I believe it was at this stage, we were on Medical Parade to receive our jabs for cholera. Not a pleasant experience, all in line with bare arm and hand on the hip, awaiting the needle. It was finally the turn of the lad in front of me and immediately after he received his, he just collapsed in a faint right in front of me. It was a shock to my system, but I managed to survive without collapsing.

Before leaving RAF North Weald, I decided to explore the nearest town, which must have been the town of Epping. Wandering around, I kept contemplating my long journey ahead to India – into the unknown and the leaving of England for the very first time. It was a quiet Sunday and as I strolled around aimlessly, I got more and more downcast. Suddenly, a house door opened, and I heard a friendly voice say, "Hello, would you like a cup of tea?" It must have been the uniform. The people of Essex were used to seeing service personnel over the previous few years, with all the airfields situated there. Of course, I accepted the offer. It boosted me and I went back to camp, ready to challenge the world!

Chapter 3
Into the Wide Blue Yonder, or are we?

January 1946. After our short stay at the transit camp at North Weald, we are close to our take-off for India. But first, we must be issued with our tropical kit. Where? The obvious choice, of course, is at Heaton Park in Manchester! It was hard to believe there was a camp in the heart of the city concerned with issuing tropical kit. However, Manchester is exactly where I received my tropical kit, including bush hat, shorts and ordinary shoes (no boots for India). The usual RAF issue of boots would be considered unsuitable for the hot climate abroad. Now that we were equipped for the tropics, we were transferred to the RAF station at Membury in Wiltshire, near Reading. It was the base for RAF Transport Command Squadrons 187 and 525, squadrons which conveyed servicemen to and from India and probably other places as well. We stayed overnight to be ready for the early take-off the following morning.

So, on Thursday 31st January 1946, reveille was at the unearthly time of 6.30 a.m. Not long after, we were sitting all bleary eyed (at least, I was) at the edge of the airfield, watching the twinkling lights at the far side and an airport surrounded by frost. We were waiting to board our plane, to start the long journey of 5100 miles to our destination, Karachi.

Our aircraft was the Douglas Dakota, developed from the DC3 and probably the most successful military plane ever, the workhorse of the RAF. It first took to the air in December 1935, on the 32nd anniversary of the Wright brothers' remarkable flight from near Kitty Hawk, North Carolina. A total of over 10,000 Dakotas were eventually in service and more than 400 still remained in commercial use in 1998.

The plaque in Heaton Park, Manchester.
No plaque for just Equipment Assistants going abroad!

Finally, we were given the order to board, strapping ourselves into our seats and all anticipating our future with uncertainty. In the midst of my reflections, an announcement suddenly came over the tannoy, "Due to a fault we will have to delay this flight."

We trooped out and prepared ourselves to do it all again whenever. The next day, on Friday 1st February, we repeated the same routine as the day before and this time there were no hitches. We actually took off from England, leaving all the years of rationing behind. I wrote a letter home about the flight, and this is it, word for word, bearing in mind that I was just 18 at the time and this was my first time of leaving home and going overseas. A big step, as anyone who experienced it will tell you.

"We took off at 0800 hours, that is 8am and there were 24 of us plus three aircrew. It was a strange sensation. The plane ran along the runway for a few seconds and we suddenly found ourselves a few feet up without knowing it. It took about five minutes to reach a flying height of a few thousand feet. The houses, fields, roads, rivers, etc. look as if they have come out of a fairy book. Nothing down there seems real. The houses look like matchboxes, trees like spots, roads and rivers look like string, although it is easier to see the rivers because they reflect. It's a world in miniature.

We are now flying over France. There are hundreds of small green squares to be seen, that is, fields. Flying almost due south, we can see occasional patches of snow here and there. So, we must be flying over the Alps now. Clouds sometimes block out our view for a while. It is freezing cold up here. Every time we want to look out through the small windows, we have to scrape ice or frost off them first. We have just had a map and a note handed round, to let us know our position and a few other details, such as the speed, the estimated time of arrival, etc. The altitude we are flying at is 8500 feet above sea level and the temperature is nine degrees below freezing point. But we each have two blankets and a greatcoat to keep us warm. The ground speed is 175 miles per hour. It is estimated that the time of arrival at our first stop, Elmas, will be 12.50 p.m. This is in southern Sardinia, near the capital, Cagliari. Estimated time of travel for the flight from Membury to Elmas is 5 hours and 15 minutes. We are cutting right across France from Le Havre in the north to Marseille in the south. It is warm there, but I doubt if it will be at an altitude of 8500 feet!

Another report has just been passed around. We are now at 10,500 feet, with a ground speed of 218 miles per hour. The time is 09.30 and we are roughly halfway across France. The temperature has dropped to 11 degrees below freezing point now.

When nearing the coast of Sardinia at 11.15 a.m., we got yet another report: 'We are unable to land at Elmas, so shall be returning to Istres, arriving there at 13.05 hours (1.05 p.m). The airfield of Istres is on the edge of a lagoon, near the large port of Marseilles in southern France. The wind is up to 90 miles per hour, which was previously behind us and helping us along, but is now a head wind!'"

At about 12.45 p.m., when the sun was rather warm and there was no cloud in view, we reached the French coast again near Marseilles. We were told to fasten our safety belts, as we would soon be landing. We were by now passing very close to Marseilles and in the near and far background there were hills. There were a lot of bays breaking up the coastline.

The Mediterranean Sea really is very blue. For the past few minutes, we have been flying over the sea near the coast, but now we are over land. A Liberator bomber flying not far away caused some excitement. We are now over the aerodrome and can see many planes lined up on the ground, which just look as big as the toy metal ones played with by my young, MUCH younger, five-year-old brother. We can just about make out people, who just look like dots on the ground. Cars and lorries appear so small that it seems you could hold them in your hand.

We have just landed in France, which was something I never expected. It appears that there are a whole series of these aerodromes dotted around the world, known as Allied Air Terminals. After a meal at Istres, the weather must have cleared over Sardinia, because we were on our way again very quickly to Elmas. We stayed overnight at Elmas, but I could only remember a couple of things about it. First, the abundance of exotic fruits (such as oranges and bananas!) after all the shortages of imported goods during the years of war in Britain. The other was when we realised that there was a cinema on camp. Wow. What luxury. A few of us lads wasted no time to go there and then found there was even no entry charge. Great stuff! We went in, took our seats and relaxed. Something was not quite right. After a short while, we realised that the soundtrack was in Italian. So, we all trooped out, never suspecting that it wouldn't be in English, all feeling slightly let down.

The following morning, we were in the air again on our way to Libya in North Africa. After take-off, a report came around. "We will land for a short while at RAF El Adem in Libya for a refuelling stop for the aircraft," (and no doubt, to also refuel our stomachs!) "then on to Palestine for a night stop." That indeed happened, as we only had a very short stay in Libya and were soon on our way again, flying over Egypt. Then another progress report. "We are unable to continue just now to Lydda in Palestine, owing to a dust storm ahead over the Nile Delta, so we are landing at Mersa Matruh for an overnight stop." We duly landed there, completely surrounded by sand and discovered we were to be overnight under canvas. The camp, with no cinema, not even in Italian, was situated in Egypt about 160 miles past the

Libyan border and the nearest place of any note was 180 miles further on, the city of Alexandria in Egypt, with abundant sand in between. What an isolated spot to be stationed in, like some airmen were. The sands at Blackpool, Bournemouth or Scarborough, OK, but this is a bit over the top!

Mersa Matruh became famous a mere three or four years earlier, being situated in the middle of the North African campaign. This was a hard-fought and complicated operation that lasted three years. Before then, it was a little-known place and apart from Matruh itself, there are other famous battle locations along the coast – namely Tobruk, Sidi Barrani and the most legendary of all, El Alamein. It was a most famous battle and a turning point of the Second World War. The two rivals involved were mainly Field Marshal Bernard Montgomery ('Monty') and Field Marshal Erwin Rommel ('The Desert Fox'). Taking an important part in the campaign was the British Seventh Armoured Division, who became known as The Desert Rats (a movie of the same name was made a few years later, starring Richard Burton). So, you could say it was one huge battle between the Desert Rats and the Desert Fox, who pursued each other along the North African coast. Eventually, there was the decisive defeat of the German and Italian forces at El Alamein, pushing them back into Tunisia, where the combined Allied Forces surrounded them and forced their surrender. A couple of months later, the Allied Forces used Tunisia as a stepping stone to invade Sicily, followed closely by invading the Italian mainland, and a very hard-fought battle all the way to Northern Italy. The whole campaign will be connected forever with British military history.

We arrived at Lydda aerodrome in Palestine (still Palestine, not to be Israel for over two more years) at midday on Sunday 3rd February. Lydda aerodrome changed its name to Lodd between 1948 and 1973, later to be known as Ben Gurion

International Airport. Actually, the camp we stayed in is not at the aerodrome at all, but at a camp six miles away. We were taken there by lorry and on our journey, we were mainly attracted to the large orange and lemon orchards on both sides of the road. There were hundreds of trees laden with both kinds of fruit. What a sight it was. For the first time we took our kitbags with us, because we would be staying for anything between 24 and 48 hours. I believe the camp was called Tel Litwinsky, which is close to Tel Aviv and surprise, surprise, we were to be under canvas again. But at least, not much sand this time. As I looked around from the entrance of the tent in the heat of the afternoon, I saw many tents and a good few white buildings like those at Elmas and El Adem. We could see the orchards not far away in the subtropical climate. At that moment, it was not very hot, perhaps just like an ordinary summer's afternoon in England, but of course, this was only early February. One minute it can be sunny, and the next it could be a heavy shower, also just like England.

The camp itself was quite modern. It included a NAAFI canteen, complete with sun veranda. The name was an abbreviation for 'Navy, Army and Air Force Institute', an organisation which provided canteens and shops for the armed forces. For a few hours every evening, there was a band playing in the canteen. There were only four musicians, but they were versatile because some of them could play more than one instrument. However, I might add it was not standard to be provided with entertainment in NAAFIs.

It also had a cinema, a fruit shop of course, a quality shop, a gift shop, a tailor shop, a barber shop, etc. The fruit shop was a favourite of mine, there was such a lot of bananas and other fruit, but also nuts. An unusual sight and the prices were unbelievable. Three oranges or lemons cost 10 mils, the equivalent of 1p! Bananas worked out at 8p per lb. Peanuts were 12.5p per lb and walnuts unshelled, 15p per lb. As with all the other countries that we have been through up to now, they would not accept English currency, so I exchanged 10 shillings into the local money. I received 500 mils for my 10-shilling note. It seemed to be a lot, but I soon found out that it was not! When we arrived in Palestine, we were told that we would be staying here for up to 48 hours, but it stretched to five days. In that time, I managed to visit Tel Aviv twice and I found it to be a remarkable city. The street names were in three different languages, Hebrew, Arabic and English. It was very modern with neon lighting everywhere. It had not been harmed at all during the last six years of the Second World War. Nothing seemed scarce there, for example, a fountain pen was 55p and silk stockings were 75p. Among other things on sale were cream and iced cakes like those in pre-war Britain. But their cost was rather high at slightly over 3p each. There were many cinemas in the town centre and numerous cafes and restaurants – all very modern and dear too. Before leaving Tel Aviv, I decided to get weighed. I put a 5mil coin in the slot and out popped a small card with my weight on it, in kilograms of course. I managed to convert it to stones and pounds, but I got a bit of a surprise when I turned the card over. I don't know why, but on the back there was a photograph of child film star Shirley Temple, famous about fifteen years earlier.

When I visited Tel Aviv at night, I was walking along this wide boulevard and although there were buildings on one edge of the road, on the other side it was jet black with nothing to see at all. Also, there was a strange sound unfamiliar to me, originating through the inky blackness. It wasn't until a long time after, that it occurred to me that the boulevard was a promenade alongside the Mediterranean and the strange noise I could hear turned out to be the surf on the beach! I would have liked to have explored Jerusalem as well, but unfortunately it was out of bounds to service personnel at that time.

From Lydda to Karachi, we flew almost non-stop for 24 hours, but we had three stops for refuelling. The first was Habbaniya in Iraq, about 50 miles from Baghdad. Construction began there in 1934 and the RAF station became operational in 1936. The west bank of the legendary River Euphrates was chosen for the location, and nearby was the Lake Habbaniya, ideal for a staging post for the Flying Boat service between Britain and India. The name Habbaniya means oleander in Arabic and it was indeed a camp of beauty, being surrounded by eucalyptus trees, hibiscus and of course, oleander bushes, all creating welcome shaded avenues. I cannot remember much about the camp, because it was only a short stop for fuel and a meal. The eminent author Roald Dahl was stationed here in 1940, which figured in one of his books, *Going Solo*. Control of the camp passed to Iraqi forces in 1955, but it was still used by the RAF until 1959, when the ensign was finally lowered. This followed a revolution a few months earlier.

The second brief stop was Bahrain. The name of this camp was RAF Muharraq, located on Bahrain Island in the Persian Gulf. The last call was Sharjah in Saudi Arabia, an airfield in use by Imperial Airways since 1932, which later merged with BOAC (British Overseas Airways Corporation), followed by BEA (British European Airways). It has been known as British Airways ever since. The RAF operated out of Sharjah from 1940 until a new airport was opened nearby in 1977 when the RAF pulled out.

We landed at Mauripur, Karachi at 10.00 a.m., or in the RAF language at ten hundred hours, on Saturday 9th February, nine days after taking off from England. We met up with most of the lads who we saw at Membury and some who flew from another RAF base in England, Bourn in Cambridgeshire.

I went into Karachi with one of the lads. There were a few cinemas and a YMCA for service personnel. But what surprised us were the little kids of about ten years old who came up to you and asked, "Shoe-shine, sahib?" or "Nice cigarette case, sahib," etc., very politely at first. They followed you around for hours and if you refused, they got a bit nasty, by throwing stones at you, trying to stick large pins in you, throwing polish, dye or anything else they could lay their hands on! We had to hire a taxi to escape them! It was a bad introduction to India, but later it turned out to be an experience of a lifetime. The taxi that we hired was actually a tonga, which is a horse-drawn carriage with two large wheels, a common form of taxi in South East Asia. Now, you can see many more auto rickshaws, often called Tuk Tuk, but the tonga is a more conventional form of horsepower transport.

There was no real need to go into Karachi because everything was available on camp. When we first arrived here, we were allocated three-tier bunk beds and I happened to get one at the top. But luckily, we were transferred to tents after two days.

The camp had two large canteens, which included a shop selling fruit, nuts and sweets. There were also a bookshop and four cinemas including an open air one. I went to the latter and it was an unusual experience, sitting outside watching a film. We are now waiting around, doing nothing in particular, waiting till we are called to our permanent camp wherever that may turn out to be. It seems that by the time we get there, it will be time for us to be demobbed! Finally, we hear that we will be stationed just outside the city of Lahore, the capital of the Punjab.

We finally left Mauripur and Karachi on 15th February, travelling on the mighty Great India Peninsular Railway, which the British initiated and was due for the Indian Government to take over at Partition very soon. Our destination, Lahore, was a journey of 753 miles and that was just across the northern part of India, a vast country. It was to take us 27 hours without leaving the train. We slept on the train or at least tried to.

When we stopped at stations en route, our meals and drinks were brought to the train by young kids who looked after us well this time, not like at Karachi! They offered a good menu, either egg and chips OR chips and egg, both swimming in grease. But the meals were very welcome, breaking up the long journey. There were of course, the 'Baksheesh, sahib,' pleas from beggars all along the route. Most just extremely young children, very distressing.

The platform at Karachi Station – the scene at the start of the journey to our permanent camp.

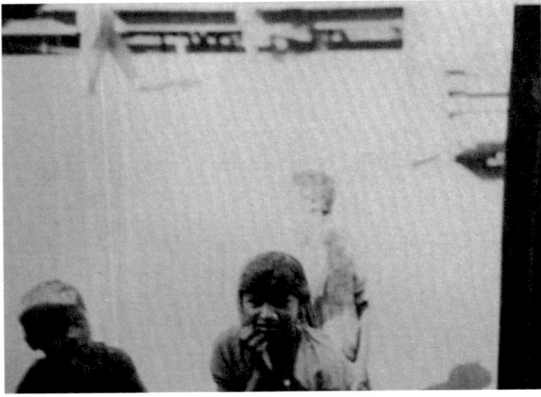

"Baksheesh, Sahib!"

We travelled across two mighty rivers and through several cities and towns on the route – the first of these cities was Kotri. Not long after, we crossed the River Indus which has its source almost 2000 miles away in the Himalayas. Shortly after traversing the broad river, we passed through Hyderabad and about 200 miles further on was Rohri (all in Sindh Province). When we reached Bahawalpur, we knew that we were just 260 miles away from Lahore and had arrived in the Punjab, our base for an unknown length of time. We were told that the name Punjab is derived from the Persian language, signifying the five rivers in the province. The name is from the Persian language but the word 'paanch' also means five in Urdu. The five rivers are the Beas, Chenab, Jhelum, Ravi and the Sutlej, all of them tributaries of the extensive Indus. Punjab, the land of five rivers. The first one that we crossed was the Sutlej whose source is in Tibet, and after a couple of hours we reached the city of Multan. Next was the city of Sahiwal, known by that name from 1966. Prior to then, it was recognised by the name of Montgomery since 1865, after the then Lieutenant-Governor of the Punjab, Sir Robert Montgomery. The last main place we passed through was the town of Okara, named after a tree called okaan, before we reached Lahore, destined to be my address for an unknown length of time in the Punjab, India Command.

We had to get accustomed to dealing with local currency. India was one of the earliest issuers of coins in the world, as far back as the late fifteenth century. The rupee, meaning 'silver', existed because originally the coins were made of silver.

Chapter 4
My home in India

February 1946. We are now installed in our new home at RAF 306 Maintenance Unit (abbreviated to MU) which is based eight miles from the city of Lahore, the capital of the Punjab, at a town called Harbanspura, on a main line railway. We waste no time to make full use of our tropical kit, the khaki outfit issued at Heaton Park, Manchester. It seems a long time since then, but it is only a matter of about two weeks.

The camp is divided into two sections. In the technical camp, there are about ten huge hangars, not for aeroplanes but containing goods and equipment destined for dispersal to camps around the area and to others further afield. There were never any aircraft on camp, and it would be difficult to entertain them without a runway! Also, the technical side included the Orderly Room, workshops, the Armoury (munitions store) and barrack stores. There were various groups of people employed here, mainly BORs (British Other Ranks, such as me), Indian Other Ranks and civilians. The domestic section of camp consisted of the cookhouse, canteen, reading room, billiard room, ration store and ablutions building (bathroom and toilet). But the greater part was taken up by the billets, about eighteen in total. Each building was about 90 feet long and divided off into three separate sections holding ten lads each, with a small room at one end for the sergeant in charge of that billet. At the front, there was a veranda along the full length of the building. This was a raised veranda of almost two feet, not sure if it was to deter possible snakes or other creatures from invading the billets. If so, it wasn't very successful, we didn't see snakes, but inside we saw all sorts of insects. And the veranda didn't prevent the flying variety, particularly when the lights were on.

Close to our new camp.

Outside the camp perimeter, with the background of one of the large hangars.

A corner of our Technical Camp.
In the Technical Camp, there is sometimes a 'technical hitch'. When the task of moving a five-gallon drum of paint doesn't go smoothly for an airman or four, the problem needs looking into!

Exterior view of our living quarters, known as our billet.

Interior view of our billet.

Apart from the insects, there were other regular visitors to the billets, such as the entertaining but cheeky chipmunks. Very similar to striped squirrels, they are fast and inquisitive. They can be very bold and in areas where they see a lot of people, they often run close to demand a treat. Also, they like to explore all interesting human things at camp.

Another regular visitor was the kite. We had a less flattering nickname for these acrobatic birds. Sometimes, after a meal we used to make a sandwich to take back to the billet, just in case we felt a bit peckish later. Leaving the canteen on our way back to the billet, we would walk side by side with our sandwiches in between us. In a flash, the kites would swoop down between us and the sandwiches were gone forever.

As usual the lads came from all over Britain, but the most popular one was Wally, who wasn't in the RAF but in the IAF, the Indian Air Force. His home was in Bangalore, way down in the south of India. At that time, it was in Mysore State, but now it is known as Bengaluru in the State of Karnataka. It is now recognised as the 'Silicon Valley' of India. Nothing stays the same! He told us many things about his homeland. I wish I could remember all the tales and stories, but one stuck in my mind. I believe his home was a bungalow and they were built on stilts to keep out unwanted visitors, like snakes. Just imagine, having to deal with snakes on a daily basis. He was useful, however, to deal with the insect 'invasion', *not* a solution that I would have used – 'squashology'! I called it 'cringe-ology'. There were some much bigger beetles built like armoured trucks, which generated even more cringe-ology. But Wally used to jump on them, without a qualm. Ugh.

A deadly, unseen enemy is the mosquitoes, but you can *hear* them. When they are close to the ear, a continual erratic zzz-zz-zzzz can be heard. We were told that malaria is not as prevalent in this area, but we still had to observe precautions as a safeguard.

We were issued with regular supplies of quinine tablets and made sure we used mosquito nets at night.

To balance the nasties, are the fireflies and glow-worms. It is a fascinating sight when they descend in their thousands on to a tree. They illuminate the tree with a mysterious greenish light. Wally demonstrated to us, if you rub one on your skin or clothes, it leaves a light of strange and inexplicable luminosity.

Also, there were many local inhabitants who come into the camp providing essential services to the personnel, such as the char wallah, the beastie wallah, dhobi wallah, pani wallah and the punkah wallah among others. Our most popular was the char wallah because he brought our char (tea) a few times a day. Very regularly (of course!) we had a visit from him. He came around with his chico (young helper) carrying the urn. At the base of the urn was a compartment containing charcoal, heating the tea above. This is where the word char came from and it gave the tea a distinctive flavour. He also carried a tin box, more the size of a trunk, containing cakes. I can't remember what kind of cakes, but certainly they and the char were most welcome at any time! Char also means the number four in Urdu, but I never got the opportunity to order 'char char'.

There was the beastie wallah who looked after the camp bathhouse. There was also the dhobi wallah who looked after the laundry and the paani-wallah who looked after the water around camp.

The most popular wallah – our char wallah with his chico.

A very useful one was the punkah wallah. His job was to sit outside at the end of the billet and pull one end of a rope, which went inside through a hole just under the roof into our room. Hanging down from this rope was a blanket and when the punkah wallah pulled on the rope outside, it moved the blanket from side to side, creating a movement of air or a draught, thus cooling the room inside.

India in general is associated with cows roaming the roads, sitting idly in the middle of a traffic jam, chewing cud of the nearest waste heap with a plastic bag tangled up in its horns. Indeed, I found it true. They had the freedom of the city and the countryside and even the camp at times. The reason why Hindus worship cows is an enigma to non-Hindus. They cannot understand why they would want to worship one of the most docile (even though they look fierce) animals in the world. It seems there are many reasons. They are a measure of wealth, they provide milk and by-products, their dung is useful year-round fuel and they are also excellent beasts of burden pulling carts and ploughs. Reveille was very early because our workday started at 6 a.m. Not so good, but the great advantage of that was that we were finished by lunchtime, here they called it tiffin. However, the main reason to start early, was to be able to finish before the heat of the day. An excellent idea. Many civilian staff were employed on camp. Apart from working in the hangars, there were also quite a few in the living quarters, helping to run the domestic site. Some of them were wallahs, the word having origins in Hindi, meaning somebody responsible for something.

Earlier I mentioned the language of Urdu, this was one of the most used languages in the Punjab together with Punjabi. English was also spoken, luckily for us servicemen, and probably because of us servicemen. However, by living and working among the local inhabitants, we did manage to pick up some of the words, such as counting. And even after over half a century,

I can still remember some of the words. I learnt to count up to about thirty, useful around camp, but only on the level of a young child:

> One (ek), two (doh), three (teen), four (char), five (paanch), six (chay), seven (saart), eight (aart), nine (now), ten (dus), eleven (gaarah), twelve (baarah), thirteen (terrah), fourteen (chaudah), fifteen (paandrah), sixteen (sola), seventeen (saatrah), eighteen (aatrah), nineteen (ooneese), twenty (beese), twenty-one (beese par ek), through to twenty-nine then thirty (teese), thirty-one (teese par ek) etc.

Following on from numbers is 'telling the time'. I can recollect just the basics. 'Bajay' translates as 'hour' or 'o'clock', so as an example, six o'clock would be chay bajay hai. It seems odd in the English language for the word 'is' (hai) to appear at the end of a sentence, but in Urdu, it always appears in that position. For a quarter to six, it is 'pohneh chay bajay hai'. For half past six, it would be 'sadi chay bajay hai' and quarter past, 'sowa chay bajay hai'.

We also picked up many useful words in the course of our days, such as sugar and milk (shakkar/doodh), OK (atcha jee), soon (tora peechee), quick or quickly (jhildee), large and small (burrah/chota), thank you (shukria).

Alcoholic drinks (beer and also possibly whiskey and other spirits) were known as puggle-paani (puggle water) an appropriate name! Paagal in Hindi means 'psychiatric disorder' and surprisingly, in Scotland puggled is slang for the state of extreme tiredness. Whilst on the subject of language, the pronunciation of Urdu and Hindi are very similar, but the written varieties are completely different. Urdu is in Perso-Arabic script and Hindi in Devanagari script. In my time in India and Pakistan, I never mastered any reading.

On camp, we met some of the veterans who had been in the Far East for five or six years and were well overdue to return to Blighty. Just imagine, if they were married, they would have been separated from their wife for all those years and if they had a baby, he or she would have been going to school before they saw them again. They used to say to us, "Roll on the boat," only they put it significantly stronger than that. It was only years after, I discovered that the servicemen were more discontent than they seemed. They, and other service personnel stationed around India and South Asia, had been on a peaceful strike lasting from three to eleven days. It started in Karachi, no more than a month before I landed in India, and spread to involve nearly 50,000 over sixty RAF stations in India and Ceylon. They were aggrieved mainly over conditions of slow demobilisation. The war had already been over for five months and they obviously wanted to get home after years away in the Far East. They had been told that British troops were being retained in India to control possible unrest during the period leading to Partition. It was good to know that our arrival allowed them to go home!

Just like these veterans, when we first joined up we all got a demob number. Mine was 69 but theirs were in the twenties. They went home within weeks of our arrival. I had a long indefinite way to go! A few years after the war, the National Servicemen were not issued with a demob number but served for a straight two years. It brought to mind, if I had been just a few short years older, I could have been in the same position as the veterans and could have been in any theatre of war. It is just fate with everyone. Incidentally, the word Blighty is an English slang word meaning Britain and is based on a Hindi word, Bilayati, meaning foreign or European.

Now that we were on active service, we were entitled to a pay supplement for 'danger money'. It seems ludicrous now, this extra payment, but it was very acceptable in 1946. We were paid the remarkable or should that be *un*remarkable glorious sum of 1 rupee a day, seven and a half pence! At the time, 100 rupees were worth £7.50 and was divided off into 16 annas and also into 64 pice, the latter only being worth approximately one tenth of a penny!

Maybe because we were overseas, we each had a free allowance of cigarettes in a tin drum containing 50, not sure if that was for a week or a month. We also received a free supply of sweets and I can distinctly remember exchanging my cigarettes to have a double ration of sweets!

Punjab temperatures generally ranged from about 117 degrees Fahrenheit (47C) in the summer to 5C in the winter. I was lucky to be posted to India in the February, because it was like a good English summer in that month and it gave me time to get acclimatised before the power of the Indian summer reached its peak. The highest I endured was 119F (48C) and *that* was hot. But it is not just the high temperature that makes it uncomfortable, humidity has at least as much to do with perspiring. I can distinctly remember when writing home. It was difficult and awkward because the sweat just dripped down my hands onto the writing pad all the time. It wasn't a case of *It Ain't Half Hot, Mum* with me. It was a case of 'It Ain't Half Hot, Ma'. With all the perspiration, it is essential to replace the moisture lost. Hot weather demands cool drinks. We were recommended to drink lime juice – not many calories and high in vitamin C. The body does not manufacture it on its own, nor does it store, so it is important to include this vitamin continuously in the diet. But avoid alcohol in the heat of the day. The temperature also created another problem. With constant sweating, the surface of the skin started erupting with a rash. This is known as prickly heat, the official name is miliaria, not to be confused with malaria, but it is similar to shingles, it is nasty and uncomfortable. It creates irritation, itching and intense pins and needles. During the hot summer months, we used to take our charpoys (beds), complete with the mosquito nets, outside for the night's sleep as it was a bit more comfortable there. But that was not without problems, because a sudden gust of wind could scatter the bedclothes around, including the mosquito net.

I discovered that there were poets on camp and I kept copies of two very good examples. I didn't quite agree with some of the sentiments in them, but I could understand why the veterans would go along with the opinions, after all their time away from home. Here are the two very good efforts, with apologies to anyone in advance for any offence caused:

The Punjab, India Command

We used to think it lousy to manoeuvre on the moors
We used to kick up hell's delight at sleeping out of doors
We thought that there was nothing worse
than kipping in a tree
And living for a fortnight on a tin of Greenwoods M and V
But now we've learned our lesson and know just where we stand
We're stationed in the Punjab India Command.

We took off one wintry morning in an icy wind that was blowing
We dreamed of bags of sunshine at the place we were going
We thought about the beaches and bananas by the score
And lots of dusky damsels like Dorothy Lamour.
But we were disillusioned, it wasn't like we planned
In this place they call the Punjab India Command.

Now, we're fed up with the tropics, we're fed up with the sun
This blasted place has browned us off, in far more ways than one
We perspire in the morning and in the mid-day heat
And when we go to bed at night, we perspire on the sheet.
All Yorkshire's lovely moors or any other brand
Would be welcome in the Punjab India Command.

So take us back to Blighty, the land of fog and snow
There's nothing really like it, no matter where you go.
We'll do without the oranges and all the stuff that's here
And all we want is Youngers or a pint of someone's beer
A stroll down Piccadilly, Kingsway or the Strand.
The natives can have the Punjab India Command.

An Airman's Lament

They call it the Garden of Eden, a gem in the sun kissed sea
Far famed for its fruit and its flowers and wonderful nectar-like tea.
They forget the savage mosquitos, the bloodthirsty dive-bombing sods
That poison your blood with diseases in this garden, the playground of Gods.

They forget the other war insects, the ant with its razor-like fang
The rats, the bats and the beetles and the rest of the murderous gang.
They forget to mention the heat rash and nights that you swelter and sweat
In the oven-like heat that enfolds you, in a power you can never forget.

They forget just where they have put us, far far away from all fun.
From cinemas, cafes and canteens. Is there no escape from the sun?
And what about all the diseases like elephantiasis and gleet, malaria, dysentery, sunstroke and hookworms that gnaw at your feet.

They call it the Garden of Eden,
A gem in the sun-kissed sea.
If this is the Garden of Eden
The back yard at home will do me.

I thought they were excellent. Who were the authors? I never found out, but it would have been someone on camp. Although there is some truth in the poems, a lot of it is exaggerated and after reading it all, I was determined to make the most of my time abroad and see as much as I could while I had the opportunity.

On camp, we had an open-air theatre which adapted to a cinema by erecting a big screen. There were more movies shown than stage shows and I remember one particular evening, when the film was Eric Portman in *Wanted for Murder*. We got very gripped by the plot when suddenly, about halfway through, the remainder of the reels were another film completely. The audience was not very happy, to put it mildly! We never saw the ending of *Wanted for Murder*, and never found out the name of the movie in the second half.

There were only two stage shows there in my time at this camp, both were put on by the Entertainment National Service Association, otherwise known as ENSA. Some thought it was sub-standard and called it 'Every Night Something Awful', but we found the two shows a most welcome break from routine.

The cast, particularly with females, had travelled out specially to entertain servicemen all over the world. There were many extremely talented entertainers and movie stars, both past and future, well known and not so well known. I can recall a play being *Nine to Five*. It was pre-Dolly Parton! I have heard that ENSA is known now as Entertainment 'N' Social Activities, who entertain at care homes, day centres, nursing homes, sheltered housing and hospitals.

For other entertainment, we used to listen to a local radio station. In our case, it was Radio SEAC Ceylon, now Sri Lanka. The initials stood for South East Asia Command and it was transmitted in English for the armed forces in India and South Asia. Radio Ceylon itself is the oldest radio station in Asia, starting on an experimental basis in 1923, only three years after the inauguration of broadcasting in Europe. I can remember one of the presenters was a young David Jacobs.

Dusk from our veranda.

I once wrote to the Radio Station in Ceylon. They were asking for stories made up of five song titles and I sent one in. I cannot remember the whole entry but it started with 'Ragtime Cowboy Joe' met 'Ramona' – two popular songs around at the time. To bring it more up to date, I have quickly devised an example based on Elvis Presley recordings:

> They met in *Macarthur Park*
> On *The Twelfth of Never*
> He said *Are you lonesome tonight?*
> She replied *Never again*
> He exclaimed *Oh happy day*

(Well, it *was* devised quickly!)

I suddenly became a DJ myself on camp for a short time. It came about like this. I unexpectedly found a limited number of records – (78s of course!) They consisted of a good selection of orchestras of the day, like Tommy Dorsey and singers like Vera Lynn, known as the Forces Sweetheart during the war. I volunteered to present some evening 'gigs', or in those far off days, they would have been known as 'music circles'. They happened occasionally, till the records were played a few times. Or it might have come to an end when the owner of the gramophone was posted away to another camp and took it with him. While presenting these musical evenings, I once organised a quiz based on the records, with a small prize for the winner. I cannot recall any of the questions, or even who won. But it all helped to entertain the troops for a very short time. Many an artist started like that while serving in the military. A very good example of this was Tommy Cooper. Whilst in the forces, he initially served with Montgomery's Desert Rats in Egypt, and became part of the NAAFI entertainment party in Cairo. One evening, during a sketch in which he was wearing a costume which required a pith helmet, having forgotten to have it with him, he reached out at the last minute and grabbed a fez from the head of a passing waiter. He got huge laughs and from that time on, Tommy Cooper and the fez became legends. Max Bygraves' real name was Walter William Bygraves and he volunteered for the RAF early in the Second World War. During concert parties, he made his name by impersonating Max Miller, which earned him the nickname of Max from other airmen and he was increasingly called upon to perform in concert parties wherever he was posted. Another well-known celebrity was Frankie Howerd, who started in entertainment during wartime service in the army, despite suffering from stage fright. But after *my* short appearance as a DJ, my entertainment career just fizzled out.

In our billet, there were talented people on camp with drawings and pin-up displays.

Drawn by Taffy, maybe of Jane Russell.

Sample of pin-ups in our billet.

Chapter 5
Lahore in the Punjab

From our camp there was what was called a 'Liberty Run', which consisted of regular transport by RAF gharrie (lorry) to the nearest large city from camp. One of the many entrances to the old city was Lohari Gate. The main thoroughfare of about three miles long in the centre was the Mall. The very pleasant, almost overpowering, heavy scent of sub-tropical plants during the warm evenings was something to always remember. The Mall seemed to comprise most of the attractions for servicemen mainly all along its route. Among some of the more well-known buildings was the Revnell Services Club, the meeting place for servicemen and women. There was also Nedou's hotel which included the Cert Club for service personnel and Government House where they held a WVS dance for the services. Apart from the dancing they offered chips, ice cream and coffee – all for the inclusive price of one rupee (8p).

The Montgomery Hall makes a perfect background for the Lawrence Gardens. This park, inspired by Kew Gardens near London, was established around the year 1862 in the centre of Lahore and named after a Governor of the Punjab of the time. In the Post-Independence era, the name was changed to Bagh-I-Jinnah. Three of us from camp went into Lawrence Gardens for a walk one morning and it was just about a comfortable temperature. We enjoyed it so much that we repeated the walk several times.

Revnell Services Club.

Lawrence Gardens with Montgomery Hall in the background.

The office of the Civil and Military Gazette was the local newspaper and occupied a most impressive building. It closed its doors in 1963 after serving the local area for 94 years.

The Lahore Museum was built to commemorate Queen Victoria's Golden Jubilee in 1887 and the foundation stone was laid by her grandson, Prince Albert Victor in 1890, who was suspected of being Jack the Ripper, like many others. One of the curators of the museum was a person by the name of John Lockwood Kipling. His son was Rudyard, who wrote the famous novel *Kim* which was set in the vicinity of this museum. The outing to the museum was very stimulating, particularly the ivory display. And extremely good value, considering that the entrance charge was only one anna, equivalent to about 2p in English currency! Also in the Mall is the University of the Punjab (the oldest of Pakistan), which was established on 14th October 1882.

The Civil and Military Gazette building.

The Lahore Museum, showing a tonga in front.

The Punjab Assembly Hall with the open space in front known as Charing Cross, fronting it is the Victoria Memorial Statue, which is now housed in the Lahore Museum, a beautiful building.

A short distance away from the Mall was a maze of streets and narrow alleyways called Anarkali Bazaar, one of the oldest surviving markets in South East Asia. It is out of bounds for service personnel during the dark hours, but I walked through it in daylight to experience the atmosphere there. It was a bustling place, full of character, with hundreds of people surging around and possibly very few who could speak English. Probably the stall holders did. I felt quite self-conscious, appearing to be the only white person there.

Right at the very end of the Mall was the Zamzama Gun or Kim's Gun. The length is just over 14 feet and the mouth opening is nine and a half inches. Its casting dates back to AD 1757. It was in fact fired in anger, the first time being in January 1761 at the third battle of Panipat, eighty miles north of Delhi and was between the Afghans and the Marathas. It has been in this location on the Mall since 1870 and it is believed that Rudyard Kipling played on it when he was a young child.

To get to know the city better, I decided to spend a ten days' leave there with two other lads. We never did any sightseeing on my first day, just relaxed and visited the Plaza Cinema. In the audience, we saw two blonde English girls and they turned out to be twins. As they would say in Urdu: Khoobsoorat Larkee (beautiful girl) or maybe Larkee Khoobsoorat – not sure. None of us managed to get acquainted with them, but we discussed them, wondering how they came to be in Lahore. We assumed that their father must have worked for the Indian Civil Service or perhaps an officer in the British Army. I saw them a few times, but the mystery of how they came to be there was never solved.

Not far from the Mall, I came across a class in progress in Sadar Bazaar.

The Zamzama Gun.

School – Indian style.

For a day trip, we three decided to visit the Shalimar Gardens, five miles from the centre, the only other one apart from the one in Srinagar, Kashmir. To make it more adventurous, we elected to hire bicycles for our mode of transport. So, we set off dodging the traffic and cows. I don't remember how we found our way, but we reached our destination without problems. It was certainly worth the effort, even though it looked a bit neglected at the time and some fountains were not working. Nevertheless, the gardens were impressive. They were the inspiration of Shah Jahan (yes, the one who built the celebrated Taj Mahal).

These gardens in Lahore were commissioned by him in 1637 and built five years later. The gardens are 500 yards long, covering an area of eighty acres and divided into three levels, so that the upper parts are concealed from the view of people entering from below. The highest, and therefore the most private, section is thought to have been used by the Imperial women. Each of the three levels is divided by canals and flowerbeds, following a Persian tradition. It is believed there is a total of 300 fountains. The gardens contain white marble buildings in typical Shah Jahani style. All are enclosed by a red sandstone wall interrupted by small decorative kiosks and cupolas. It all adds up to a very pleasing and restful ambience. Too soon, it was time to depart and mount our bikes once more. The return journey started off OK, but about halfway the pedal crank on my bike started working loose and after a few minutes, it was hopeless to ride. What to do? We ended up by me riding on the crossbar of one of the other bikes and the third member of our party rode his bike, wheeling mine alongside. We were all parched with thirst by the time we got back into the city centre.

Shalimar Gardens, Lahore (1).

Shalimar Gardens, Lahore (2).

At the very end of the Mall is a road sign – a reminder of home.

One evening, we went to the Cert Club downstairs in Nedou's Hotel. They were holding a dance and included were some novelty ones, such as an elimination quickstep and a ten-second waltz. The Commanding Officer of our camp was there for a while. In an interval of the dancing, they arranged a contest between two teams, four lads against four girls. It was in the form of a spelling bee. In spite of the lads' team captain not misspelling any words, the girls' team won by two points.

July 1946. There have been reports of communal tension beginning to rise in the area, due to the expectancy of the forthcoming partition of the sub-continent, but I have not witnessed any of it yet. It seems we are away from it on camp.

Chapter 6
Imminent End to an Era

Saturday 8th March 1947. Just over five months away from Partition.

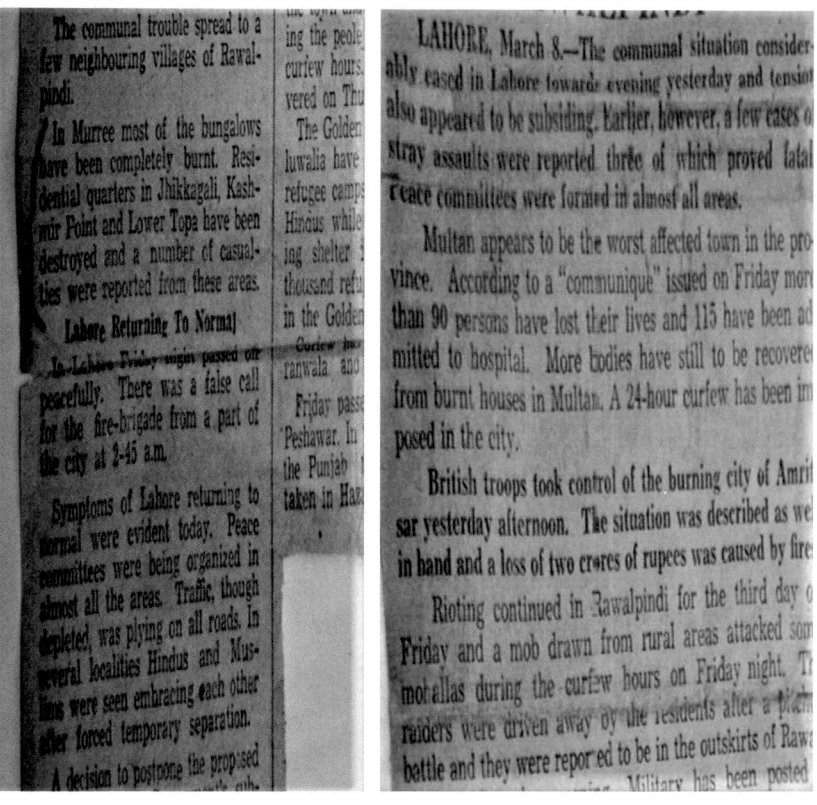

Saturday 8th March 1947 – Reports in *The Civil & Military Gazette,* Lahore.

The *Civil & Military Gazette* is a local newspaper published in Lahore and founded in 1872. Rudyard Kipling, the famous author born in India, (of *Jungle Book, Just So Stories* and *Kim* fame) joined the staff of the Civil & Military Gazette in 1882 and was asked to contribute his collection of twenty-eight short stories in a publication called *Plain Tales from the Hills*. He stayed for five years as assistant editor, after which he moved on to the sister newspaper at Allahabad.

Thursday 17th April. We experienced a big fire at our camp. Not arson but caused by combustion because of the excessive heat. Massive columns of dun-coloured smoke rose thousands of feet in the air. Eleven fire engines battled furiously for five hours before the fire could be localised and brought under control. A fire officer reported that the fire might continue to smoulder for another three days. He said, "we are trying to keep the temperature below ignitable point in order to prevent the fire from spreading further." The gutted depots stored clothes, boots, valuable aery-parts, petrol, lubricants and what is called 'dope' a highly combustible paint. It is mainly lacquer applied to fabric-coated aircraft. It stiffens and strengthens the fabric stretched over airframes. With model planes it is often applied to reinforce tissue paper. The terrific heat of the conflagration caused stocks of these five-gallon drums to explode with a terrific noise sending them high into the air. The fire altogether embraced an area of approximately 20,000 square feet. Seven adjoining hangars were saved, so the firemen did a great job in the circumstances. Providentially, there was no loss of life. But for a brief time, there were 'human-shaped' smoke markings on one wall. However, no one was reported missing, so we were lucky that there were just a few casualties sustaining slight burns. But the loss in property was a different matter, as that was conservatively estimated at two crores of rupees, about one and a half million pounds.

Top: Emptying the ammunition store – a hazardous operation.
Bottom: A corner of the paint (dope) store with the five-gallon drums.

General scene at the height of the blaze.

A 'saved' hangar.

While all the excitement on camp and plans for reorganisation were going on, I received orders for an escort duty to Karachi in the Sindh Province of northwestern India, departing in four days' time. I would miss some of the action while I was away. Also, I would have the opportunity to 'cool off' a bit. A temperature chart published in the local newspaper, showed the Lahore temperature to be 109F and the Karachi reading to be only 106F. Great, three degrees cooler. Something to look forward to!

Monday 21st April 1947. I got up early this morning to make final arrangements for escort duty on my own to Karachi. I was to be there for six nights, reasonable and satisfactory because the train journey would take twenty-seven hours each way. I would have time to unwind between the journeys. My escort duty consisted of, not to accompany a person as I expected, but to deliver the kit (belongings) of a serviceman with the surname of Kessell. Not much to go on. I collected the necessary chitis (forms) and proceeded to the MT (Motor Transport) Section, at just after Aart Bajay Hai (eight o'clock). At nearly Pohneh Now Bajay Hai (quarter to nine), they finally found a gharrie that worked and after picking up my kit and also Kessell's, we set off for the station in a 15cwt Chevrolet lorry. At the train, I couldn't find a berth for myself in the military section, so the ticket collector found me one in a civilian compartment. Somewhere between Montgomery (now known as Sahiwal) and Multan, the train stopped at a station possibly at either Chichawatni or Kanewal. Along the platform, and also travelling on the same train, I spotted a familiar face from camp, Flight Sergeant Parsons, who was on the way for some leave in Karachi. I joined him for the rest of the journey. He informed me that my berth had been claimed at Lahore by someone else, but that there were still unoccupied berths in this compartment.

My berth had been taken by an RAF lad from Scotland and he was on his way to a posting at Drigh Road RAF Depot, now

Pakistan Air Force Base Faisal. His demob number was the same as mine, 69. So it was obvious that we joined up the same time and will also be demobbed together. It's a small world.

Tuesday 22nd April. The train was still thundering (an ideal descriptive word) towards Karachi when I woke up, but it was not until 11.30am that we arrived at Karachi Cantonment. I discovered that the temperature reached 106 degrees Fahrenheit in Karachi yesterday, but I got off lightly because it attained 109F in Lahore. The Flight Sergeant said he was booked into the British Union Jack Club and would see me there later. I reported to the RTO (the Railway Transport Office for the Forces) and they rang through for transport to take me to the RAF General Hospital. This is run as a separate unit and I was informed that there are about 200 BORs (British Other Ranks) stationed there. My transport came very quickly, an ambulance!

Arriving at the Hospital, I went to the Wardmaster's office, but they found no trace of Kessell in the patients' book there. Now that's a good start – what to do next? First job was a spot of tiffin, as it was time for lunch. In any case, I couldn't enquire further until 14.00 (2pm), when the Orderly Room (basically the Camp Office) reopened. Success! The elusive Kessell was in the records and I was told that he was currently on a course at Drigh Road RAF Depot. Accordingly, I left the kit with the QM, his full title Quartermaster, who specialises in supplying and provisioning troops, the equivalent in the Navy is the Purser. Of course, I got a receipt for the kit, proof of delivery.

I travelled by tonga to the British Union Jack Club and booked in for five nights. I wasted no time and went across the road to hire a bicycle for a look around the town. I rode around mainly to see the shopping centre and of course, the cinemas. I booked for the evening presentation at the Paradise Cinema and the ticket cost no more than the equivalent of 10p. What's more, I discovered that the seats were sofas and easy chairs!

Paradise Cinema.
It could be a cinema in Britain, but it had nineteen large electric fans suspended from the ceiling in the auditorium.

Wednesday 23rd April. Soon after breakfast, the Sarge and I went for a cycle ride to Clifton Beach on the shores of the Arabian Sea. It was the first glimpse of the sea since I was posted to Lahore fourteen months ago. We experienced a dip in the sea, but we were disappointed. It was not 'pukka' sand, meaning not real sand, more like mud. However, remember that was over sixty years ago and I've heard since that the Defence Housing Authority or similar Government Organisation have since been filling the beach with real sand and the resort is now the most popular picnic area at Karachi.

Thursday 24th April. In the morning, I went to Karachi City Station to reserve a berth for my journey back to Lahore in three days' time. Then I called into the YMCA and found out there was a sightseeing run in the afternoon. I put my name down for it. However, before then there was some spare time so I collected my bathing trunks and, together with the Sarge, we made our way along Queen's Road, aiming for the Union Jack Bathing Pavilion at Chinna Bay. We couldn't find it and ended up instead at the Merchant Navy Club. Yes, they let us in, regardless of the fact we had no connection with the Merchant Navy. At this stage, I couldn't swim, learning would come later. But even if I could, I doubt if I would have swum, because there was a very strong current running and it was twelve feet deep. That did not deter the friendly sergeant. He was a powerful swimmer. After swimming for a while, he noticed a diving board. It was all of thirty feet high and was willing to have a go. He climbed the ladder, reached the top, launched himself off in a perfect dive, disappeared under the water for a few seconds, came to the surface, swam on the double to where I was standing and exclaimed, "Never again!"

At four o'clock, I went back to the YMCA to join the guided trip. It cost me all of 10p and was to a place called Mangho Pir where crocodiles can be seen, about seven miles north of the city.

The transport was by 15cwt Chevvies (again). There were two vehicles in our group. The journey was through some hilly country and it reminded me of the Burma Road in miniature – not that I have ever traversed the Burma Road. My impression was only based on photographs. The region has hills of between 700 and 800 feet, somewhat picturesque, with occasional glimpses of the level plains beyond.

The hot sulphur springs at Mangho Pir are believed to have curative powers. I tried the water and found it to be very hot, not surprising with the surrounding air also being very hot. This locality claims the oldest shrines in the area, possibly 700 years old. But the main attraction to me on this particular trip was the crocodiles, an integral part of the shrines. I estimated wrongly that there was a total of forty reptiles. A report estimates hundreds enclosed in a walled area measuring about 400 feet x 200 feet, with the water distributed by an underground stream. They were reputed to be originally pets of the Pirs (Islamic scholars or Holy men) at the Shrines. The crocs I saw were offsprings of those and supposed to be very tame. Fascinating creatures, but I wouldn't trust them. They looked vicious, to me.

Crocs at Mangho Pir.

This trip must have been X-rated, because after the ferocious-looking crocodiles, our next call was to be even more frightening. It was to a leper colony. It is a place of quarantine for leprous people and is greatly feared by the general public, because it is highly contagious and incurable. Leprosy causes disfigurement and disability. There were many distressing sights there, with human beings crawling about with no limbs. But despite all that, they appeared to happy in their own way. I didn't know what I was letting myself in for when I booked this outing, but it is good to be faced with reality sometimes and very sobering.

The return journey was, like the outward journey, through gentle hill country in the Sindh Province outside Karachi. It was interrupted by a break in the hilly country for refreshments. We were all provided with a cooling orangeade and a cake, most acceptable in the circumstances, as it was still very hot.

Friday 25th April. This afternoon, we left the Union Jack Club to go to Manora, an island in Karachi Bay, where it is said that one could get a good swim, or in my case a good dip in the Arabian Sea. Manora or Manoro is just a small island south of Karachi. Together with the neighbouring islands, it forms a barrier between the city of Karachi to the north and the Arabian Sea to the south. The island is connected to the mainland by a narrow strip of land called the Sandspit, about seven and a half miles long. The journey consists of two stages. overland transport to the docks at Keamari. First of all, we had to get to Preedy Street, where there were two choices of conveyance, bus or tram. The island was accessible by the conventional ferry, by motor launch or more interestingly by Bunder Boat taking about fifteen minutes.

The fourth (and last) alternative was more uncommonly used as a ferry, a military DUKW, more popularly referred to as a 'duck', a six-wheeled amphibious landing craft equally at home on land or water. The more conventional use was for storming beaches at the time of battles. As it was such an unusual mode of transport, we decided on the 'duck' for the watery part of our journey. However, there was no sign of it when we arrived at the port, so we opted for the ordinary ferry. I got the impression that Manora Island is about three or four miles long and contains a lighthouse 91 feet high, established in 1851, a 'legacy' of the British.

The mangrove forests in the background merging with the long, sandy beach gave the scene a secluded beauty, with the lighthouse adding to a quaint feel of the island. Strictly speaking, it is not an island, because to the north, the beach merges with the beaches of the Sandspit and extends even further to another resort, Hawkes Bay. On the Manora beach itself, I found the breakers very large and continuous. This would be expected, being exposed to the Arabian Sea, which leads in turn to the massive Indian Ocean.

There was a cantonment (military section) on the island of Manora with married quarters, patients convalescing from the RAF General Hospital and leave personnel. Furthermore, it also contained a reasonably priced canteen and even included a cinema. For our return to Karachi, this time we managed to coincide with a military launch, the 'duck'.

The crossing back to the mainland on the 'duck' took twenty minutes, twice as long as the motor launch, but lots more thought-provoking. We also changed the mode of transport on the land section of our return journey. By catching a bus, it cut the journey by half, compared to the tram on the outward ride. Very unadventurous!

Saturday 26th April. We enjoyed our trip to Manora yesterday, so we decided to repeat the experience once more, particularly as it was my last full day in Karachi. We still felt unadventurous because we travelled both ways by bus. However, on the way back from Manora, this time we tried the bunder boat. It was well worth the participation, and a fitting climax to my escort duty in Karachi.

Sunday 27th April. My last day, and I spent most of the morning packing and writing. Flt. Sergeant Parsons had to go to RAF Mauripur today. He was not at the British Union Jack Club when I left there and it turned out that we were never to meet again.

On the DUKW or 'Duck'. The author is standing in the centre of the picture.

Leaving Keamari on a bunder boat, which is similar to a dhow…

…but on which two sure-footed boys clamber along a plank extended over the side, to keep the craft on an even keel.

Saturday 17th May 1947.

Report in the Civil & Military Gazette.

This report went on to say that the situation in the walled city of Lahore took a turn for the worse on Friday noon when rioting spread to the entire area between the Taxali and Yakki Gates, including where disturbances occurred on Thursday evening. About half a dozen persons were reported to have been stabbed in the area since the morning, four of whom succumbed to their injuries. Many other areas were involved in stabbings and arson attacks including Mohalla, Chowk Wazir Kahn, Chohata Mufti Baqar, Chohata Basti Bhagat and Sarin Mohalla. Thursday night was more or less peaceful after 9.30, due mainly to the intense patrolling by armed police. Troops had also been patrolling around Lahore city since Friday morning. Several fires were raging in three parts of the city at 2 p.m. on Friday. One person was stabbed in Old Anarkali by a passing cyclist. Panic prevailed in the city.

Tuesday 3rd June 1947. It is now over a month since the escort duty to Karachi and the clock is ticking unremittingly towards the partition of the huge sub-continent. The Mountbatten plan has reported today that a deal has been made for all participants concerned and the target will be 14th and 15th August. This plan is so complicated with so many factors involved – religious, political, cultural, historical and territorial.

Thursday 26th June. For a while now, the local population have been studying the sky and exclaiming, "The monsoon is due on the 28th." They seem to know or sense the deluge. It wouldn't be before time, because the heat is becoming unbearable and it would be a great relief when the rains arrived. The perspiration pours off, even when you do nothing. When you try to write a letter home the sweat just runs down your fingers onto the writing pad. The temperature has reached a peak of 119F (48C), quite enough for me.

Saturday 28th. The summer monsoons roared in today. How did the residents know? But they did! The winds carry moisture from the Indian Ocean and bring heavy rains from June to September. We 'British Other Ranks' were very grateful as we jumped about in the rain to cool off. It almost fell horizontally aided by the strong, uncontrollable winds. Luckily, there was very little damage on camp, but the torrential rainstorms often cause violent landslides elsewhere. Entire villages have been swept away during monsoon rains. Despite the potential destruction, they are welcomed in India. Farmers depend on the rains to irrigate their land. Additionally, a great deal of India's electricity is generated by monsoon rains, so a lot of good often comes from the bad.

Monday 30th June. Around this time, I went in for a test for the next stage in my promotion. I passed and I am now a fully-fledged LAC (Leading Aircraftman). Very impressive, but that's the highest rank I reached.

A report today announced that we are to be posted to the RAF Camp 301MU at Karachi by 8 July, in preparation for leaving India. This, however, was proved to be wrong, because I still had my most stimulating, thought-provoking, fascinating and, most importantly, life-changing experiences ahead of me before I departed India's shores.

I didn't have long to wait for my first experience. At one time today, I had practically walked the full length of the veranda at the entrance of my billet when I stopped abruptly. No! I froze. There, just a mere four feet or so away, its raised head a few inches above the veranda step, was a cobra. No, not just a cobra, but a king cobra with its head extended ready to strike. The species are very venomous and can inject up to two-tenths of a fluid ounce of venom, enough to kill twenty people. In a flash, my mind hurried through my past life, short as it was. Time stopped. Neither moved, aggressor or victim. Nothing moved for a long time, it seemed, but was probably only a few seconds. I remember thinking that king cobras grow on average thirteen feet in length and have been known to reach eighteen. I cannot recall how long this specimen was, but I believe the bulk of the body was hidden below the veranda. Neither did I recall hearing the bone-chilling hiss like a growling dog. My mind was numb, but eventually, of all things, I was suddenly aware of a sound behind me. Automatically, I turned my back on the menace in the front and discovered a lad laughing behind me. Between laughing, he was also speaking. It took some time for it to register what he was saying. Eventually, I heard him explain, "It is a real king cobra, but only a stuffed one, a souvenir belonging to one of the lads in our billet." I didn't tell him off, nor did I feel annoyed with whoever left it where he did, because I was so relieved.

Throughout the months of June and July 1947, there had been increasing accounts of unrest escalating into violence and rioting in the Lahore area. Inter-communal violence between Hindus and Muslims became endemic. We had been out on the rifle range practicing. The two may be connected, fearing the worst. It was about then that there was an announcement stating that British troops (I assume they meant British forces, including RAF) would commence to leave India on 15th August. But in the meantime, despite all the menace of the continuing violence due to the impending Partition, we servicemen and women surprisingly appeared to be able to continue with our normal routines on camp.

One of my pastimes was visiting the cinema in India and I was very surprised to find them all showing American and English films. Wherever I went, Karachi, Lahore, Delhi, Agra, Murree and even in the village of Jhika Gali, I found cinemas with English soundtracks. Not like at Elmas in Sardinia on my flight out to India, where the talking on screen was in Italian. That seemed such a long time ago. Since then, I had experienced many wonders and incidents, not on the screen, but in the real world of India, with many more to come. More than I could have thought possible. Time was very short now to 15th August and Partition.

However, it was with sheer nostalgia that I recollected the films I had seen whilst away from Blighty's shores. Averaging about one a week, I had seen many a landmark in the history of the cinema. Several films come to mind for 1946/7, probably the more important ones were:

The Conspirators, with Hedy Lamarr and Paul Henreid.
Anchors Aweigh, with Gene Kelly, Frank Sinatra and Kathryn Grayson.
Rebecca, with Laurence Olivier and Joan Fontaine (the first production in America for Alfred Hitchcock).
Keep Your Powder Dry, with Lana Turner, Laraine Day and Susan Peters.
State Fair, with Jeanne Crain, Dana Andrews and Dick Haymes.
My Favourite Blonde, with Bob Hope.
Andy Hardy's Double Life, with Mickey Rooney and Ann Rutherford.
Night and Day, with Cary Grant as Cole Porter and Alexis

Smith as his wife.

Bathing Beauty, with Esther Williams and Red Skelton.
Blue Skies, with Bing Crosby, Fred Astaire and Joan Caulfield.
Jungle Book, not the cartoon which arrived 25 years later. This version starred Sabu.

All these were American, but there were some British stars too, such as James Mason, Stewart Grainger, Phyllis Calvert, Patricia Roc, Jean Kent and Margaret Lockwood, to mention just a few household names of the time. All these and many more were authentic 'film stars'. My first reaction would be that in the present age, they are mostly unknown and long forgotten. But with the advent of television, many of the old, some might say antique, black and white films are resurrected again and again for the present-day audiences. There were also the regular, familiar faces in the 'bit parts' in films. The list would be endless, but just a few as they come to mind, Edward Everett Horton, Sheldon Leonard, Guy Kibbee, Franklin Pangborn, Edward Arnold, Eve Arden. There was also an actor who always played a drunk on screen. I always remember him staggering about and talking gibberish. I can still remember what he looked like, thinning and displaying a moustache. However, I cannot recollect his name.

Whilst on the subject of movies, it was about this time I received a letter from home. My young brother, now seven years old, was taken to see a Western called *The bad men of Missouri*, and he called it '*The bad men of misery'*.

During the summer of 1947 there were reports of communal rioting, due most likely to the impending partition of India. It was a complex problem, with so many aspects involved. Provinces, princely states and language played a part in the gigantic jigsaw puzzle. If possible, all had to lock together to achieve separate objectives. But by far the most important consideration was religion. There were three main factions. For the Hindus, there was Jawarhalal Nehru and Mohandas Karamchand Gandhi (more widely known throughout the world as Mahatma Gandhi), Quaid-e-Azam Muhammed Jinnah for the Muslims and the third to take into account were the Sikhs, prominent with them were Master Tara Singh, Giani Kartar Singh and Sardar Baldev Singh. There were reports of communal rioting during the summer. One evening, I was in Lahore and just after coming out of the Plaza Cinema I realised that the Mall was without streetlights and there were noticeably more Punjabi police about than usual, all carrying batons. One was holding a rifle. Then we heard chanting and along the Mall came a mob stretching the full width of the road and pavement. The police were in line waiting for them. What happened next was unpredictable. The police grabbed a few of the leaders and deposited them into a Black Maria parked nearby. We learned afterwards that they were dumped out in the countryside, to cool off while walking back to town! And the rest of the mob soon dispersed.

Tuesday 1st July 1947. The report of 30th June has been countermanded. Instead of being posted west to Karachi towards Blighty, my destination has been changed. It was a matter of go EAST, young man, NOT West. We were to be transferred soon to RAF 308 Maintenance Unit at Allahabad which is 500 miles short of Calcutta to the east of India and coincidentally 500 miles further away from Blighty when the time comes. Before leaving India, it seems the British Forces are possibly being moved away from the Punjab, which appears to be the main region of the horrifying clashes.

Tuesday 3rd July. We transferred from Lahore camp after being stationed there for fifteen months and were installed at Allahabad RAF Camp. And this was just over a month away from the upheaval of Partition.

Coincidentally, I moved from Lahore to Allahabad exactly sixty years after Rudyard Kipling did precisely the same move, but he went from one newspaper office to another – *The Civil & Military Gazette*.

Monday 7th July. We spent some time on the rifle range again today. It was announced that there would soon be three air forces on the sub-continent: Indian, Pakistani and for a short while, Royal as well.

Sunday 13th July. In today's Routine Orders, details appeared about the Hill Party in the foothills of the Himalayas and this would be for my second stay to cool off from the oppressive heat of the plains. All on the list, about 24 of us had to be prepared to leave "almost immediately." To refresh my memory, it was in regulations that all service personnel were to have a period in the hills to cool off from the plains of India during the summer months, I went the previous year in June and I didn't mind in the least getting re-acquainted with the glorious Murree Hills area again.

Thursday 17th July 1947. It was reported that all British personnel will leave India by 15th August. That was rather optimistic for us when very soon we were going to the Hill Station. Last year we stayed in the hills for nearly three and a half weeks. Routine Orders announced that the Hill Party would join the 'Frontier Mail Train' on Monday 21st July and was due to depart from Lahore Station at 10.30 hours. The destination was Rawalpindi on the first stage of our journey into the hills. That would mean we would be due to return from the Hill Station very close to the Partition Day itself. However, going back to Lower Topa made me recall my very first visit there.

Monday 21st July 1947. Now for our second stay at Lower Topa. We were taken by gharrie (RAF lorry) to Allahabad Station in good time to catch our train. I very rarely witnessed any violence, rioting or crowd trouble relating to the forthcoming

Partition. But on the station platform whilst awaiting the departure of our train, we witnessed someone being led off by a group of people. They took him out of the station, but we dared not interfere. It has been on my conscience ever since. 10.30 hours, the Frontier Mail left on time, because the express train only took six hours to reach Rawalpindi, compared to the sixteen hours last year. The message of this tale is to pick a MAIL train when you can! Just as we were arriving at Rawalpindi, it started raining very heavily.

At 16.30 hours, it was still raining when the train stopped. Luckily, there was a gharrie waiting for us at the station and we soon piled on. Off we went on our forty-mile trip up to Lower Topa, making a quick call to RAF Chaklala Air Base to pick up a few more passengers before leaving the Rawalpindi area. 19.45 hours, it took just two and a quarter hours, experiencing and enjoying the mountain roads en-route. There was even a meal waiting for us, so the journey all worked out okay for us this time. We 'celebrated' our arrival at the hill station, by attending a second house performance at the camp cinema!

Tuesday 22nd. Some of us were anxious to see the town of Murree again, so six of us set off on a little expedition along the bridle path, and about a mile from the town it started to rain very heavily. We sheltered for a while under trees, but got so wet, we decided to return to camp in the rain, because we could get no wetter!

Wednesday 23rd. Had a stroll to Jhika Gali with Ken, to re-acquaint myself with the charming little village.

Friday 25th. Today, we decided to aim for Murree again. But this time we didn't attempt walking there, not chancing rain like the other day, but went by local bus. Apart from a bit of shopping, Ken and I risked a walk up to Kashmir Point at the northeastern end of the ridge on which the town of Murree is situated. It is reputed to be the highest spot in the area and from there can be seen a panoramic view across the valley of the River Jhelum and on into Kashmir to the Pir Panjal range of the Himalayas. It was very tantalising looking at the mountain ranges stretching into the distance and I said to Ken, "I would like to go into Kashmir for a few days." He agreed, so we decided to apply for some leave and to enquire about the possibility of arranging a few days in Kashmir.

The town of Murree, by day and night...

…and sometimes obscured by cloud.

Main Street in Murree.

It was already getting dark on the way back to camp from Murree. The headlights on the bus kept going on the blink. Quite unnerving, particularly when it coincided with seriously sharp bends on the mountain lanes. In any future trips to Murree, I'm not sure whether to risk the buses or the rain.

Tuesday 29th. Ken and I went to the Orderly Room and Guard Room to enquire about leave and visiting Kashmir. We were issued with a chiti (a letter or note) giving us permission to be away from camp tomorrow until 5th August. As a result, we hired bikes, ignoring buses and risking the rain. We cycled to Sunny Bank, a suburb close to Murree, to book our seats on the bus for Kashmir. And so that was the start of an amazing trip of only five short days, but which was destined to remain vividly in my memory always and maybe change my life forever.

Chapter 7
First day in Kashmir

Wednesday 30th July 1947. After tiffin at Domel, 45 miles travelled with 110 miles still to reach our objective, Srinagar, we continued on our way north towards Muzaffarabad. When we were within a few miles, our bus turned sharply to the right in a south-easterly direction, with the River Jhelum now on our left, into the heart of the Pir Panjal range, a part of the Himalayas which divides the Kashmir Valley from the Indian State of Jammu. Passing through a small village called Garhi, we eventually arrived at a place named Chenari (or Chakothi) where we had just reached the halfway mark on our journey between Lower Topa and Srinagar, 76 miles. At the time, it was only a matter of eight miles of road to travel to the next place, Uri. But soon, due to Partition, I had heard that this bus service (Rawalpindi-Srinagar Bus Company) was due to close. The border between Indian Kashmir and the newly born Pakistan Kashmir would be at a bridge between the villages of Chakothi in Pakistan and Uri in India. After Partition, it would be more difficult to pass between the two countries. Initially, it meant that travellers would have to make a long detour via Delhi and Lahore – a five-day trek! However, there appeared to be agreement between the two governments on humanitarian grounds for Kashmiri nationals to travel more freely to visit their families on both sides of the bridge. It was said that bringing the two sides together would never have been possible without this bridge. In the old days, before power-driven vehicles were available, the journey from Murree to Srinagar was divided into eleven stages, each of ten to twenty miles. Bungalows were built at regular intervals for travellers to spend the night or change the horses. It must have quite an experience then. It still was! Our bus continued on its way through Uri and Chakothi, the route followed the winding rapids of the River Jhelum. Our route stayed on the right bank all the way now through to Srinagar. This terrain is very mountainous, wild, rugged and the road was mostly narrow, with passing places. What I think is that it is amazing that even though a lot of the route was virtually single track, we always met oncoming traffic (not that there was very much!) at passing places. I'm sure the drivers had no telephones to contact any vehicles approaching.

And all this time, our route was following the course of this turbulent river and gradually rising in altitude from the lowly 1938 feet at Kohala, to the lofty 5200 feet above sea level at Baramula, at the opening up of the Vale of Kashmir.

The wild Jhelum and the mountains topped by snow in July.

Baramula across the River Jhelum from our bus.

The Vale of Kashmir.

We are now just thirty-three miles away from our destination, Srinagar, the capital of Kashmir, near the other end of the Vale. Baramula has an old name, Varahamula which was derived from early Sanskrit. The region is strikingly scenic, with the mountains (which we have just traversed) to the west and the open valley (towards our destination Srinagar) to the east. Baramula is also known as the Gateway to Kashmir, even though we have already travelled in Kashmir for about a hundred miles. Known as The Valley, the fertile Vale of Kashmir itself is a remarkable area. Although it is one mile above sea level, almost all around the rim of the valley, the surrounding mountain ranges tower above by a further several thousand feet.

Now in the Vale of Kashmir, the river has changed its mood. It has turned tranquil and placid, featuring a shikara, the Kashmiri version of the Venetian gondola. About halfway along the Vale, we pass through the village of Pattan, historically known as Shankarpur, the last main village before reaching Srinagar.

Finally, we reach our objective, Srinagar, the capital of Kashmir and the largest city. Also known as the Venice of the east. It has also been the summer capital of Kashmir for years. The name comes from Sanskrit. Sri means 'wealth' and Nagar translates as 'city'. The city is divided into two parts by the river Jhelum. Yes, it's the same river which our route followed for just over 130 miles from Kohala, where the bus entered Kashmir.

I usually pronounce Srinagar to almost rhyme with vinegar, but by no means is it sharp. I believe it is pronounced 'Sree Narga'. It is an attractive and serene part of the world. A lake, a garden city and a gateway to the most beautiful parts of the great sub-continent. And not quite fifty miles further upstream from Srinagar is the source of this prominent river Jhelum, at a place called Vernag.

The view close to our hotel, The Mount View.
The road on the right (Boulevard Road) follows the shore of Dal Lake
around to the Shalimar and other gardens.

We checked into our hotel, just a modest guest house really. The proprietor, Mrs Sharmer, turned out to be an expatriate from Britain, in fact from Scotland. I was sure she would be useful to us for language and advice during our stay. She greeted us with, "Welcome to Kashmir. Do you know where you would like to visit during your stay with us?" Ken and I let her know that, whilst in Kashmir, we would like to visit Gulmarg. It is a hill resort famous for its legendary beauty, both in summer and winter. We had booked five nights in Srinagar and she said, "We have a Mount View Hotel there and you can spend one of your nights there, instead of here, if you like."

"That would be great for us," Ken and I exclaimed together. So, we decided to have our first two nights here in Srinagar and booked Friday for one night's stay in Gulmarg.

Next followed the usual check-in conversation about times of meals, etc. She informed us that dinner would be served at 7 p.m., but not extended like in the bigger hotels, and breakfast was from 8 a.m. to 9 a.m. I glanced at my watch and announced that we will have time to visit the Shalimar Gardens before dinner.

Ken asked if she was here in Kashmir on her own. "Oh, no. I have a husband, he's Hindu and we've been married since 1930. We have two children, a girl of sixteen called Lotus and Anand, a boy of twelve. He is a fine boy and helps when he can, but our daughter is at an awkward stage. She helps sometimes here in the hotel, but she cannot be relied upon. She's a wonderful girl, some of the time. She has teenage tantrums and has a mind of her own and sometimes doesn't listen. She's naive and as innocent as a lotus flower. That's our Lotus! She is named after the lotus flower which is the symbol of beauty, grace, purity and serenity."

"In spite of all that, she sounds like someone to avoid," I commented.

"You can find out for yourselves at dinnertime. She is due to help – if she turns up."

Ken and I looked at each other and I said, "Thank you Mrs Sharmer. We'll set off now for Shalimar. Where can we get a taxi?"

"Just the short walk to the main road, Boulevard Road, and they come along frequently."

After thanking her, we took the short walk to the main road and hailed a passing taxi. The route follows the edge of Dal Lake around to the Shalimar. The ride took us through splendid scenery. After travelling about ten minutes or so, we reached our destination and entered one of the most famous gardens in the Kashmir valley. It is situated overlooking the shores of the serene Dal Lake. The word 'Shalimar' means 'abode of love' in Sanskrit, the world's oldest language. Therefore, the house of love was built by Mughal Emperor Jahangir for his beloved wife Nur Jehan more than 400 years ago. The lush green and well-maintained Garden of Srinagar was designed with terrace lawns, fountain pools and combined with mighty chinar trees and pavilions. The garden is composed of four terraces in which the topmost terrace was originally reserved for the royal ladies and is considered to be the most beautiful section. We walked by a long fountain pool to the pavilion at the end, entered it, turned around and looked back along the full length of the fountain pool. The entire scene felt sacred and divine, with high mountains framing the background.

Suddenly we heard the sound of giggling over to the right. Outside the pavilion were three girls, two of whom were facing us. The third had her back to us and I noticed she had flowing jet black hair almost down to her waist. Just then she threw an empty bottle of coke down on to the path. I don't usually lose my temper, but almost without thinking I blurted out, "What are you doing? Have you no respect for these beautiful gardens?"

She turned around, rather startled at first, then it changed to an expression of annoyance and she glared at me for a few seconds then turned away and walked off. As they went, I noticed all three were dressed in a kameez (a long shirt) and shalwar (baggy trousers). She was in red and I also noticed she carried a red shawl to match her outfit. They all wore colourful pendants and long dangly earrings. Then they were gone.

After a quick last look around, Ken and I decided to come back the next day for a more leisurely visit to the garden. We then made our way back to the hotel in time for dinner, arriving back with a few minutes to spare. Just enough time to spruce up a bit for the dining room and we sat down at our table a couple of minutes before 7 o'clock. There were about four other tables occupied and the waitress was serving them. Suddenly I noticed she had jet black hair almost to the waist. She was the girl I shouted at in Shalimar. She could be the daughter, Lotus.

Whilst she was going back and forth serving, I was studying her eagerly. I noticed that she had pale hands and skin, not a round face nor a long face but more oval, blue eyes to match the lakes of Srinagar, a cute little turned-up nose, delicate pink lips and blushing red cheeks like the lotus flower. Now that I can see her properly, I thought this was a girl I could spend the rest of my life with! I asked myself, could it be love at first sight?

It was time to serve our table. Ken and I both said together, "Hello, pleased to meet you, Lotus."

She turned to Ken. "Pleased to meet you too. Mum tells me that you are from England."

"Yes," he replied, "but we are stationed with the Royal Air Force at Lahore at the moment. We are here to spend just a few days in Kashmir, starting with a longer visit to Shalimar tomorrow morning."

She gave him a sweet smile. 'Wow', I thought. But she ignored me completely and turned to continue serving. A short while later I heard her call out to her mum, "I'm going to see my friends for a while," and off duty she went.

After we finished eating, I said to Ken, "I don't think she was very happy with me.

"That is an understatement," he declared. Then he suggested, "Should we have a walk alongside Dal Lake to see the area on foot and also to walk off our dinner?" I agreed, and we set off on the short walk and turned to the right into Boulevard Road with Dal Lake on our left. It was an interesting stroll on the winding road with the lake on the left and some houses on the right interspersed by greenery, with a background of mountains. We had only travelled a few minutes when the road curved to the right, passing a longer stretch of bushes and trees on the right, the opposite side to Dal Lake. Just then, I heard a low sound coming from behind them.

I turned to Ken, "Did you hear that? It sounded like someone whimpering."

"Yes, you're right. I heard it too. Should we investigate?"

I gave a brief nod and we rushed through a gap and stopped in surprise. There was a girl stretched out on the grass with a man pinning her arms down with his knees and another man at the girl's head holding her arms also with his knees. He had already lifted her kameez above her waist and was moving his arms downward.

All this happened in a few seconds and even without realising it, I had clenched my hand into a fist. I rushed across at the same time, let fly and my fist connected with his chin. The aggressor fell back, shook his head, got up speedily, then rushed off. At the same time, Ken, who is a much bigger build than me, rushed over to the other one. He saw Ken coming, hastily got up and followed his fellow conspirator off the scene. The girl was still sobbing quietly.

It was then that I noticed that she had long, jet black hair! And then realised where she was from. What a coincidence or Fate. "Let's get you home. Relax now. You're safe with us."

With Ken one side and myself the other, my arm around her shoulder with mixed feelings, we guided her back to the hotel and found her mum, who took over. We told her what had happened. She thanked us for our help and guided Lotus away gently.

Reflecting later in bed, I thought that amazingly I met Lotus three times in just my first day in Kashmir. Is that Kismet? I asked myself. What a day. Such a lot has happened. What else could be in store?

Chapter 8
Second Day in Kashmir

Thursday 31st July. One o'clock in the morning. I heard Ken get out of his bed to 'pay a visit' and thought that he was rattling around a bit. I turned over and went back to sleep.

In the morning after our first night, I commented to Ken, "You got up in the night."

"No," he said "it wasn't me, but it seemed if someone was walking about. I thought it was you." Strange.

"In that case who was moving about? A burglar?" We didn't know and went down to breakfast wondering how Lotus was after her ordeal.

Mrs Sharmer greeted us. "We are so grateful for what you did yesterday. Thanks to you both, Lotus is a lot better this morning."

"We were so fortunate to be there in time."

"She'll be down soon to thank you personally." She turned away then turned back. "By the way, did you feel the earth tremor in the night?"

We were both astounded by that. So, we didn't have a burglar in our room. As I previously mentioned, the whole area was (and still is) prone to earthquakes. We considered ourselves lucky that it didn't develop this time!

As we sat down for breakfast, Lotus came into the dining room and immediately approached our table. She acknowledged both of us. That was a great improvement for me after yesterday's encounter. We asked her how she felt after a night's sleep.

"I feel good, thanks to you both. You acted very quickly and I am indeed very grateful what you did in the circumstances."

All the time she was talking, I was noting that her voice and accent were perfect, with a very charming combination of her mother's Scottish accent blending with her father's Hindi accent. And I thought, is this girl perfect in every way?

"Can I ask you something?" she said hesitatingly.

"Anything you like," I said.

"Can I come with you both as your guide?"

"A good idea, when can you be ready to go?"

"In just a few minutes. Breakfasts are almost finished. There are several gardens such as Chashme-Shahi, Nishat Bagh, Harwan and Shalimar, whichever you like."

"With not having enough time to give them all justice, we would prefer to spend longer at Shalimar than we did yesterday." I added, "It was the place where we first met. It was a real special occasion for me."

She gave her little giggle then looked down shyly. The giggle sounded better than the first time I heard it at the pavilion at Shalimar and it reminded me what happened yesterday.

Not long after, we arrived at the garden and Lotus wasted no time in acting as our guide: "The world-famous Shalimar Gardens, renowned as the monument of love." Another modest look down. "Constructed by the great Emperor Jahanjir in approximately 1616, for his beloved beautiful wife, Nur Jahan. It comprised four terraces with flowing water and almost 150 impressive fountains. These gardens were inspiring enough for a poem and a song about them. The poem was written originally by Laurence Hope. No, not male. The name was the pseudonym of a woman by the name of Adela Florence Nicolson. Music was added by another woman, Amy Woodforde-Finden, and thus was born 'The Kashmiri Song'. There are two Shalimar Gardens in India and it is not certain on which one the poem or song was based. The one here in Srinagar is more likely with its title, but Nicolson living in Lahore added some weight to that notion."

In an encyclopedia I looked up a long time after, I found that several movies featured 'The Kashmiri Song'. Among the more well-known where the song was either mentioned or sung were: 1) Rudolph Valentino in the film *The Sheik* in 1921, and 2) Deanna Durban sang it in *Hers to Hold* in 1943. However, the most popular time for the song was around the piano within drawing rooms of early twentieth century England and it remained popular until the Second World War. It is a beautiful old song.

The Kashmiri Song

Pale hands I loved beside the Shalimar,
Where are you now? Who lies beneath your spell?
Whom do you lead on rapture's roadway, far,
Before you agonise them in farewell?

Oh, pale dispensers of my Joys and Pains,
Holding the doors of Heaven and Hell,
How the hot blood rushed wildly through the veins,
Beneath your touch, until you waved farewell.

Pale hands, pink tipped, like lotus buds that float
On those waters where we used to dwell.
I would rather have felt you round my throat,
Crushing out life, than waving me farewell.

We wandered around the gardens, possibly for almost two hours, under the capable guidance of Lotus taking us through the terraces with all their fountains and eventually entered the pavilion where we were first destined to meet. Something on my conscience urged me to speak.

"Lotus, I have realised since yesterday here that your giggle is," – I thought briefly – "cute, but yesterday it was in an inappropriate place and I apologise completely for the outburst.

It's not like me at all."

Lotus responded thoughtfully, "I realised later that it was not the right place to act like that and also with the empty bottle. It is almost a sacred place. I apologise and I accept your apology."

Ken was listening to all this, and suddenly came out and said, "That's a relief. Why don't you kiss and make up?"

There was an embarrassing silence between us. I broke it by saying, "Let's continue our guided tour, but it is lunchtime now. Would you like to join us for lunch and manage to come with us to the Hari Parbat Fort atop the famous hill overlooking Dal Lake? It sounds an interesting place to visit for the fort and the view."

"Thank you and yes I would be happy to escort you to Hari Parbat."

And then we very reluctantly left the Shalimar to go for tiffin.

The Shalimar Gardens, Srinagar.

Hari Parbat Fort.

During our lunch, I said, "I have heard many girl's names: Rose, Lily, Iris, Violet, Daisy, Poppy, Nigella, Hyacinth, Petunia, Myrtle, Jasmine and probably others, quite a list, I but have never heard of Lotus."

"My dad named me that because the first time he saw me soon after I was born, he noticed my blush red cheeks and I reminded him of the lotus flower. That's what he told me a few years after, when I was old enough to understand."

"Yes," I said, "that was one of the first things I noticed about you when you turned around yesterday, but you were not happy with me just after I had lectured you."

"That is all forgotten now after what happened later. All that is forgiven," Lotus continued, "however, back to my given name. It is Ramapriya, Rama means Goddess of Fortune or good luck and Priya means dear or beloved."

Thoughtfully, I commented, "I could agree with that, but that doesn't cover your beauty."

She glanced down again briefly but didn't reply.

After the lunch, we soon arrived at the foot of the hill ready for the climb up to the Hari Parbat Fort and Lotus gave us the introduction to the historic site.

"It is a six-hundred-foot climb above the lake. This historic stronghold is believed to have been built during the eighteenth century by an Afghan Governor Atta Mohammad, but a long stretch of the walls seen around the hill was constructed in 1590 by the great Mughal (yes, yet another Mughal) Emperor Akbar. From the summit, the views of Dal Lake and parts of the Valley are spectacular."

As we neared the summit at a steeper part of the path, I was in the lead. I turned and saw Lotus closely followed by Ken in the rear. I held my hand out and Lotus took hold of it. I felt a sensation, but not sure if she did. But we both paused briefly without saying anything. Then we continued on to the Fort atop the hill. We enjoyed giving it respectable time viewing the Fort and admired the view of Dal Lake, the surrounding valley and encircling mountains. By then, it was time to make our way down to the hotel.

Later on, after dinner, Ken and I went into the hotel lounge and there were just two couples already in there relaxing after dinner. As we walked over to two seats, leaving another one available next to us hoping Lotus might join us, I noticed something on a table in the corner. When I got closer, I realised that the object was a record player, together with a small collection of records. I took a quick look through them and discovered they were easy rhythms to dance to.

When I sat down next to Ken I said, "They have a record player over there. Do you dance?"

"No, not really. Do you?"

"Well, I haven't danced much, but I can manage to get around the floor OK. I thought maybe to ask Lotus, if she comes in here tonight."

Just as I said it, she came in and sat next to us. I didn't want to ask her straightaway about dancing, so I said, "You have mentioned that all forenames have meanings. Do Hindu surnames also mean something?"

"Yes, of course," Lotus replied, "for instance our family name is Sharmer and in Sanskrit it means joyfulness, comfort and happiness."

"The meaning still leaves out beauty for you," I observed.

Lotus smiled and continued, "The Sanskrit language is the oldest language of ancient India and in fact goes back 3500 years. But my father's language, Hindustani, is a more recent one and is spoken widely in northern India and around Delhi. The other main language of Northern India is Urdu. Both languages essentially sound the same, but in writing they are very different. Language in the Indian sub-continent is a very complicated thing."

"It sounds very complicated," commented Ken and after a pause he continued, "changing the subject Lotus, I'm curious to know, a girl like you must have a lot of admirers?"

Coyly she answered, "I'm not sure about that, but there is one boy I like. He's in my class at school and is a few months older than me. Dad doesn't like me mixing with boys, because he thinks I am too young yet. Can I change the subject?"

Comments came quickly. "Of course," and "Would you like to ask something?"

"Tell me what England is like, because I've never been further than Delhi in my life."

"I'll answer that, Ken. I think there mainly three things to say. Firstly, in England people mainly keep to themselves, but when someone has a problem, they rally round to help. Secondly, we almost always talk about the weather. If it's raining, when is it going to stop. Or when it isn't raining, when is it going to start!"

And finally, there are plenty of delightful and interesting places to visit. These comments may be a tongue-in-cheek answer."

"What is the tongue in cheek?"

"It is a bit of a jokey answer, but it is basically true," and I went on to remark, "Lotus, sometimes you seem to be a naive little girl and sometimes like a woman of the world knowing such a lot. But that's why I enjoy being with you."

We all thought about that for a while. Ken glanced at his watch and commented, "It has just turned ten o'clock. I'll turn in. There's another busy day ahead of us tomorrow in Gulmarg. We are only here for a few days and want to pack in as much as possible. We'll want an early start to make the very most of our few days here in Kashmir. Good night, both."

We both acknowledged him as he left the lounge.

There was a brief silence between Lotus and me, then I asked her, "Have you ever had a holiday in Delhi and Agra?"

"I've never been outside India, but yes I have visited both," she confirmed.

"Ken and I went there a few months ago and we found them to be very interesting destinations and with many examples of Mughal architecture, particularly the Taj Mahal, our main reason for visiting the area."

Putting on her travel guide voice, she said, "Yes indeed, the Mughal Empire lasted for 381 years and left a great impression here in India. After that, Britain took over in 1857-58. Now Britain plans to bestow independence and partition after ninety years of rule."

There was silence for a short while and I remembered the dance records.

"Do you dance, Lotus?"

"No, I've never ever had the opportunity."

"Would you like to try it now?"

"Yes, I would, if you will show me how."

"I will start a record and then I will show you."

I put a record on the turntable. The song was called 'Dream, When You're Feeling Blue', composed by Johnny Mercer and performed by a group of singers called The Pied Pipers.

"Are you ready?" I asked, approaching Lotus, "First we have to stand close."

We both stood up and faced each other with a small gap.

"Next, I raise my right arm and you hold your left hand in my hand. I put my left arm around your shoulder and your right arm goes around my waist." We remained like that listening to the music. Time seemed to stand still, but it was probably just for a few moments.

"Now take a step back in time with the music and I'll take a step forward." We started to move together, with me guiding us around slowly.

I noticed that a couple had joined us on the floor. Lotus and I were both concentrating on keeping up with the music and moving around the floor. I then got a little braver and spoke to her, whilst she was concentrating. "This is great. It's like floating on air and you are doing very well for your first time."

"Yes," she replied. "It is like a real illusion. When I feel sad, I will remember this."

"A Real Illusion?" I commented. "That is quite a contrast, but I know what you mean."

When the music stopped, the other dancers chose the next record. Lotus and I just waited close together, getting closer until the next tune started. We then started moving around slowly.

"Since the very instant that we first met, I have wanted to do this." With that, I raised my hand and touched the crown of her head and gradually lowered it down her back through her long, jet black wavy hair all the way slowly to her waist. I looked at her face and saw she had her eyes closed.

When she opened them, we held hands and walked slowly upstairs to our rooms. When we reached the bedroom landing, we paused for a brief while until the feeling was decreasing.

I said, "Oh, a thought just occurred to me. I wrote a diary about when Ken and I experienced our visit to Delhi and Agra. I have the diary in my room. I could get it for you if you like. It's with some photos I took at the time."

"Yes, I would like that."

With that I rushed into my room and very swiftly I came back to Lotus and handed her my diary.

"Here it is and I have named this episode 'In which I have a mainly Mughal Journey'. I hope you find it interesting. I'm sure you have seen and know all about the places we explored."

"Most likely and I will read it before I sleep," she replied with a giggle, "and it will be like a fairy tale from you."

"I hope you enjoy it." We went slowly to our bedrooms

holding hands and I left Lotus at her door. On the way to mine, I thought that after dancing close together I reckoned that she was about four inches shorter than my five foot six. It must be because she was slim and curvy that she looked taller.

Chapter 9
In which I have a mainly Mughal journey

Mughal – a member of the Indian Muslim dynasty of Mongol origin, who ruled large parts of India from 1526 to 1857.

February 1947 has arrived. Lord Louis Mountbatten has been appointed the last Viceroy of India. At the same time, it was announced that the British would be out of the Indian sub-continent by June 1948.

The amazing Christmas is just a memory. Ken, from Hayling Island near Portsmouth, occupies the charpoy (bed) next to mine in the billet and between us we decided to visit Delhi and Agra, so we applied for a fortnight's leave. Ever since we put in for this leave, we expected it to be cancelled for one reason or other. First, the shortage of BORs (British Other Ranks), because a lot of them have been repatriated back to Blighty and very few are being posted to India with the imminent event of Partition. But I believe the main reason to be the rioting, which has spread across the sub-continent. Until the very last minute, the leave could easily have been cancelled, but...

Friday 7th March. We went to the Guard Room to enquire if there was a gharrie going down to Lahore Junction and were told that one was leaving at 12.30 to take civilian drivers there. The Adjutant said that we could catch the train from Bombay, which was scheduled to leave Lahore for Delhi at 13.45.

So, everything was settled, or so we thought. It was not to be as straightforward as that. At about 12.15, a lad came off duty and told us the gharrie was cancelled! We had just finished connor (tiffin/lunch) at the canteen and were prepared for the journey. So we rushed back to the Guard Room and on the way, we saw two other lads, Fred and Roy, which turned out later to be a big stroke of luck. Fred said to us, "If there is no gharrie available, come and see me." We found out that the next transport going into Lahore was at 14.00 hours, missing the Bombay train and it would mean roughly twelve hours' wait near the station, where maybe a riot may break out. We went to see Fred and managed to find him just after one o'clock. Ken and I had already given up the idea of catching the 13.45 Bombay train. Fred came back to us at 13.20 and told us to get to the M.T. Room (Motor Transport Room) right away. We had already taken our kit a few minutes previously. Just before we reached the M.T. Section (Motor Transport), Paddy drove up in a gharrie and told us he wouldn't be long. He drove round to his billet and came back a few minutes later with an *escort.* There was Mervyn in the passenger seat of the 15cwt lorry, something like a jeep, and three other passengers in the back. Paddy shouted to us, "Jump in quick. We haven't much time if you want to catch your train." He was actually going to try to reach the station before the Delhi train left! We went round to the Officers' quarters to get the 658 form signed. We had to follow procedure, even when short of time.

As we set off, I noticed that it was now 13.35, which left us just ten minutes to get to the station! We were now hoping the train would leave late. What a ride it was! Paddy did the run in a record ten minutes. It is hard to believe that in my diary at the time, I had written that the journey normally takes about 25 minutes! In the short drive, I gathered my thoughts and suddenly noticed that the lads were prepared for trouble. We had quite an armament on board. Paddy, our driver, wore a pistol around his waist and the other three held Sten guns. However, there was no trouble. We hadn't much time to contemplate the potentially risky situation, but we had travelled down in a virtual armoured truck and upon arrival at the station, we had been 'dumped' among hordes of people, who may have been planning to riot. At nineteen years of age a person is a daredevil, but when older, just wouldn't even consider doing these things.

The train left at 14.00, so we caught it in good time and managed to get a full seat to ourselves. The rail part of the journey was quite a normal one, except for a few minor episodes. As we passed through Amritsar, we noticed that plumes of smoke were rising from the direction of the city. An aircraft, believed to be a Dominie (a twin-engined biplane), was circling the area and dropping leaflets. It caused quite a bit of excitement to all, among the locals on the station platform. The Ludhiana episode started at five o'clock at Jullunder Cantonment where we ordered eggs, chips and char for the next stop, which was Ludhiana. When we stopped there, a chico (young boy) brought our order straight to us. We tucked in, but when we were halfway through it, our real order turned up! After about thirty minutes protesting, we saw that we would have to accept this pukka (genuine) order as well. It was only later that it occurred to us that it could all have been planned. At least we were sure to have eaten enough, double portions of egg and chips.

Saturday 8th March. We arrived at Delhi at 2.10 in the middle of the night. Delhi was the old Mughal capital and was reinstated in place of Calcutta, by Imperial declaration as capital on 12th December 1911 by HM King George V. In 1947, it was a city of just over half a million people, altitude 709 feet above sea level. But to me at the time, I found Delhi as the tale of two cities. Not like in the novel of Charles Dickens, which is really about two cities – London and Paris. But Delhi is about Old and New Delhi. More of this later. From the station, a bearer showed us the way to the Wavell Club, almost opposite.

There had obviously been rioting earlier in the night, because sadly on the way, we noticed a couple of bodies along our route, not yet claimed by family. Being only eighteen, we never thought to dwell on them. Fear comes with age.

When we arrived at the Wavell Club, we retired almost immediately at about 3 a.m. It had been a long and tiring day. Not that we had a full night's sleep ahead of us, because we arose at just after nine o'clock. The newspapers reported that Lahore was almost back to normal again and was 'out of bounds' to service personnel. It should be OK by the time we return from leave. Also reported, was that Amritsar and Multan were burning.

And here we were, in the midst of it all, ready now to explore Delhi. First, even though the Wavell Club was a very pleasant and modern place with its own swimming pool, it was situated a few miles outside the city near the railway station. So, we decided before starting our sightseeing, to look at some of the Service Clubs which were more in the centre. We hired bicycles to go into the city centre, passing some of the places we would return to later. Among the important Delhi highlights on our route were the Red Fort, Jama Masjid, Delhi Gate, Firoz Shah Kotla, India Arch. We cycled along Kingsway and at the other end was the Secretariat and the Council Chamber. All these locations we would have to revisit when we had more time to explore. In the meantime, we continued our ride and passed All India Radio. Then soon after, we arrived at Connaught Place, near where the Red Shield Club is situated, our base in Delhi. We booked in and had lunch there, before returning to the Wavell Canteen for our kit. When we arrived back there, we handed in our bikes and had refreshing iced coffees and showers. Then we hired a tonga to take us and our kit back to the Red Shield Club. This journey turned out to be our longest tonga ride, taking around 35 minutes altogether. By now it was 17.00 hours (5 p.m). It was just by chance we happened to be in our room and we discovered that every evening at the same time, a chico brought tea and sandwiches to all rooms. After finishing the unexpected snack, we began our sightseeing close by. It was to Connaught Circus and Connaught Place, the main shopping area of New Delhi, built in 1931 and believed to be modelled on Royal Crescent in Bath, England.

This hub of New Delhi is a vast traffic circle. The outer circle is the 'Circus' and measures around one and a half miles, with the inner 'Place' being almost half a mile in length. The latter is also known as Rajeev Chowk. To add to the traffic confusion, there are seven streets radiating from the middle. There is a uniform series of colonnaded buildings devoted to shops, banks, offices, restaurants, hotels and cinemas, of which the latter are four in number, all in English: The Plaza, Rivoli, Odeon and Regal. Very English and I'm sure all have been renamed long before now. We visited them all at various times during our stay, along with regular forays around the Circle and Place. We had our lunchtime meal at yet another Service Club, the Allied Forces Canteen. The fellow who supervised it was very useful. He had been based in Delhi for a while and advised us about the places to visit. One of the places he mentioned was very nearby, the Jantar Mantar, so we decided to make that a morning call tomorrow. We were in for a weird and wonderful experience.

Connaught Place shopping colonnades.

In the evening, we went to a cinema and I had an unfortunate episode there. Everything went OK until the end of the main feature. We stood up to follow the rest of the audience and started walking towards the exit. For some reason, I felt in my rear pocket in my trousers and to my dismay, my wallet wasn't there. I know that it is a silly place to keep it. But I have *never ever* left it there since that day. I went back and looked around my seat very carefully, but there was no trace of it. The wallet had either dropped out of my pocket somewhere or was removed gently, very gently. There had been a lot of money in it – 100 rupees, all gone. In sterling, that worked out to nearly £8! We were only at the beginning of our leave and Ken loaned me some of his money until we got back to camp. Luckily, he had enough for both of us and we scraped through the remainder of our trip. And it never put us off the enjoyment of all our sightseeing to follow.

Saturday 8th. From the Red Shield Club, it was only a short walk through Connaught Place to the Jantar Mantar, also known as the Delhi Observatory. It is an ancient structure in the heart of New Delhi, a clash of cultures, it seems. But it is amazing and mind-blowing, a masterpiece of Indian architecture. It was built by Jai Singh the Second, of Jaipur, early in the eighteenth century and took almost seven years before the whole structure was fully operational, to make sure of the accuracy of the various instruments. It shows the scientific wisdom of ancient India. It is a structure which consists of fourteen geometric devices used for measuring time, forecasting weather changes and predicting the behaviour of planets. The largest device or instrument is the Samrat Jantar which is 56 feet high, the base around one hundred feet long, and its shadow plots the exact time of day. In other words, it is a massive sundial. From the top is a bird's eye view of two round structures which measure the sun and moon. These two round buildings behind one another are for measuring the sun and moon respectively.

The whole structure is made of stone and marble and it acquired the status of a national monument in 1948. It has always attracted architects, historians and scientists from all over the world.

Jantar Mantar Observatory - the giant sundial.

Structures for recording Moon movements.

Monday 10th March. This morning we hired bicycles for the whole day and initially aimed for the Red Fort (Lal Qila or Lal Kot). The foundation stone was laid in 1639 and the massive building was inaugurated in 1648, at the very peak of Mughal power, by Emperor Shah Jahan. (Yes, the very same who built the legendary Taj Mahal). The fort was built in red sandstone, giving the fort its name, and it is indeed mammoth in size.

The perimeter walls are about one and a quarter miles long. They vary in height from almost 60 feet on the Yamuna River side and practically 110 feet on the city side. The moat, with no water since 1857, is 32 feet deep and was originally crossed by creaky wooden drawbridges, but these were replaced by more reliable stone bridges in 1811. The main entrance is through the Lahore gate and through the appropriately named Naubat Khana, because it translates to Welcome Room. Also in this area is the Naqqar Khana, the Drum Room, also a suitable name, because music was played there five times a day.

Within the fort, there are many courtyards and pavilions, just one of which is the impressive Diwan-I-Aam (Hall of public audience) in a large courtyard, in white marble and with dimensions of 80 x 40 feet. It was a hall used for audience with dignitaries and foreign emissaries and contains an ornate throne for the Emperor. It was featured in a painting in the Bodleian Library Oxford, showing Emperor Shah Jahan receiving the Persian Ambassador in 1628. However, there is some controversy about this, because the archives show that this date was before the fort was built. Also impressive is the Diwan-I-Khas, which was used for the Emperor's private audience.

The main entrance to the Red Fort.

The Lotus fountain, which sprays not only water but scent as well.

Leaving the Red Fort the same way we came in, through the Lahore Gate, directly opposite is a famous Old Delhi street. But first we have to negotiate a busy junction in front of the entrance to the Fort. Right in the middle, is a policeman on traffic control. With his aid, we manage to reach the other side and enter Chandni Chowk. This is one of the oldest and busiest markets in the city. The name means Moon Market Square, but it is not really a Square, it is a long street running through the middle of the walled city.

Originally, there was a canal, part of the water supply scheme, which ran alongside the street and it is said that moonlight reflecting on the water, earned the street its name, chandni (moonlit). It wasn't always the street of bustling markets. During the Mughal Dynasty of Emperor Shah Jahan, when entering Delhi, it was the route on which he made his way leading his luxurious procession to his place of residence, the Red Fort. That period of his reign only lasted a very few years.

By now, it was lunchtime (tiffin time). In the afternoon, being very close by, we visited the Masjid-I-Jahan Numa. The Urdu translation means 'Mosque commanding a view of the world', probably because it is situated on high ground. It is one of the largest and most famous mosques in India and is more well known as the Jama Masjid.

Building started in about the year 1642 and took fourteen years to complete. The creator was Emperor Shah Jahan (similarly to important mosques at Agra, Ajmer and Lahore), but this one is the largest of all. Built mainly of sandstone, it contains three domes of black and white marble, the domes reputed to have taken 5,000 masons five years to build. The mosque has two minarets, both of which are 130 feet high. On arrival, we went through the usual procedure and left our shoes at the entrance – very safe. Also, it warned not to have bare arms and legs. We were both OK in that respect.

Outside the Red Fort.

The Courtyard of the Jama Masjid.

The courtyard was mind-blowing, it can hold up to twenty-five thousand worshippers. Not far away was the Wavell Club, so we went there for a shower and a cooling drink. Then we returned our bikes to Connaught Place.

Tuesday 11th March. After our long, hot, day of sightseeing and riding in the heat on Monday, we agreed to take things easier for a few days. We had been to the cinemas frequently to relax a bit since we arrived and we discovered that for the time being, we had seen all the films on at all four cinemas. So, we had to find alternative ways of relaxing and passing the time between our forays into history. Consequently, we took to playing table tennis and darts. For some reason, we had to supply our own table tennis balls. We even tried the table-top football machines in the service clubs.

Monday 17th March. We hired cycles for the whole day to delve again into ancient, and some up-to-date, history. We aimed south from Connaught Place, about seven or eight miles in the Mehrauli district of the city to the Qutab Minar. On the way, we passed quite a few places of interest, including the Jantar Mantar (visited previously) and the imposing double Secretariat buildings.

These two sandstone structures were built during the 1920s by a leading British architect of the time, Edwin Lutyens, who designed the Cenotaph in London's Whitehall in 1919. These New Delhi buildings were given a typical oriental look, each being topped with a chatlis (similar to a tall pagoda). These twin buildings are known as the North and South blocks, used for the Civil and Military respectively. They are now the seat of the Indian Government and are used for the Ministry of Finance and the Ministry of External Affairs. The four columns in front represent Australia, Canada, New Zealand and South Africa. To one side, the prominent circular building is the Council House. Situated in between the Secretariat blocks and built in 1929, is the

Rashtrapati Bhavan with its three hundred rooms, now the residence of the President of India. Directly in front, towards the east and flanked by the Secretariat buildings, is the start of a main thoroughfare called Kingsway, now known as the Rajpath. It is a broad avenue, with open spaces and green parks. We cycled along its full length, about a mile, and there very noticeably straddling Kingsway, is the India Gate (or arch) containing the King George V statue and the All India War Memorial, which pays homage to Indian soldiers who died during the First World War, the Afghan Wars and in the North West Frontier. It was also designed and built in 1931 by Edwin Lutyens. The arch is about 130 feet high. It is situated in the middle of a roundabout and is very reminiscent of the Arc de Triomphe and the Champs-Elysées in Paris, except there are no shops lining Kingsway. We retraced our steps along Kingsway, back towards the Secretariat and just before reaching it, turned left to travel in a southward direction, down the Safdarjung Road and past the old Willingdon Airport (now Safdarjung Airport), to explore the Qutab Minar complex.

The Qutab Minar.

This ancient site is made up of many components, of which two particularly caught my eye and mind. The main draw I found was the centrepiece, the Qutab Minar itself. It is a soaring tower about 240 feet high with a girth around the base of 47 feet, which 'shrinks' to 8 feet at the top and consists of five storeys. Known as the tallest brick minaret in the world and the tallest monument in India, it was started in 1192 and has worn remarkably well.

I managed with effort to ascend the pillar and counted a total of 390 steps to the top, but it was worth the climb because the view from there was amazing – mile upon mile in all directions. The perfect bird's eye view over Delhi. The tower has been compared to the Eiffel Tower in Paris and to the Leaning Tower at Pisa in Italy. Perhaps the latter is more accurate because, like the Leaning Tower, is beginning to lean out of true – about 25 inches. It is sometimes known as the Tower of Victory, dating from Islamic rule in India, but is also thought to be a tower for prayer by the Muezzin (priest). Another quaint, bizarre reason for the tower, for some people, is the belief that it was built by somebody called Prithviraj Chauhan, so that his daughter could behold the sacred River Yamuna (Jumna) from its top as part of her daily worship. Quite an imaginative notion!

In contrast to Qutab itself, the other attraction is only 22 feet tall, or to be precise, only 22 feet showing above the ground. It is the astonishing iron pillar in a courtyard on site and it shows no sign of rusting, after it was erected in the *fourth* century. The whole complex is a popular spot for the citizens of Delhi.

After lunch, we had a change of direction, we headed to north Delhi. On the way, we spent a short time at another ancient attraction. When we reached massive walls and three gateways, we were aware we had arrived at the Purana Qila Fort.

The Kashmir (or Kashmiri) Gate, through which the British stormed the city during the Mutiny in 1857.

The Afghan ruler, Sher Shah, who briefly interrupted Mughal sovereignty by defeating Humayun, completed the Purana Qila Fort during his reign (1538-45) before Humayun regained control of India. But not many years later, in 1556, Humayun lost his footing descending the stone steps at a tower here and sustained injuries from which he later died.

We continued our journey north to St. James Church and Kashmir Gate, with just a half mile between them. Both were prominent features in the Mutiny days and the siege of Delhi on the 14th of September 1857. The oldest church in Delhi, construction began in 1828 by a man called James Skinner, the son of a Scottish father and a Rajput mother. He was badly injured in a war in the early nineteenth century and promised if he survived, he would build a church in commemoration of his faith in God. His grave is still in the church, in front of the altar. The church was badly damaged, sustaining many bullet holes in the dome, and the ball and cross at the top were also spoilt. It underwent renovation in 1865. Nearby is the Kashmir Gate built in 1835, so named because it was the beginning of the road to Kashmir; a long way off, at least 200 miles, but not far in Indian standards. To this day, evidence of the battle is visible on the existing walls, damage due no doubt to cannon balls.

On our way back to the Red Shield Club for the night, we called at yet another place of interest in the area, Firoz Shah Kotla. This was the imposing citadel of the fifth city of Delhi known as Firozabad, built in 1354 by the great builder and Emperor Firoz Shah Tughlaq. Two other interesting facts emerge from this site, an old one and a modern one. The old one certainly qualifies for ancient. It is an iron pillar that is 2197 years old and about 42 feet of it shows above ground. It was there in 1947, so I would imagine that it would have survived another few years and this particular one has survived better than some others. Known as Ashoka's Pillar, it reminds us of Emperor Ashoka, probably the greatest emperor of all time.

A more modern-day fact of Firoz Shah Kotla would be recognisable to cricket fans, because nearby is the famous cricket stadium established in 1883. Although I wasn't aware of its proximity at the time, only about a year later it staged their first test match, for the season 1948-49. It is one of the premier grounds in India.

Tuesday 18th March. Today we walked a mere mile to the west of Connaught Place and came to the elegant Birla Mandir Temple also known as the Lakshmi Narayan Temple. With its soaring spires, the tallest reaching to 165 feet, it was built in cream marble and red sandstone. It was constructed by industrialist B.D. Birla and opened in 1939 – a modern building in the land of ancient structures. The help of 101 skilled craftsmen was utilised, creating a masterpiece in stone over a period of six years. It was inaugurated in that year, by none other than the Father of the Nation, Mahatma Gandhi, on the condition that all castes, especially untouchables and other faiths, would be allowed in. There are many Hindu Gods represented in this sacred shrine, the main ones being Vishnu, the supreme God, and his consort Lakshmi, Goddess of prosperity and good fortune. And surprisingly, within the complex is the Geeta Bhavan, a Buddhist temple housing frescoes of Buddha. The great world religions of Hinduism and Buddhism philosophy are loosely connected through Karma, very hard to clarify. One explanation is: "The quality of somebody's current and future lives, as determined by that person's behaviour in this and previous lives." Now we know, or do we? Perhaps the simplest and briefest way is to say that people are judged on deeds done in this life. The whole of the Birla complex is a curious, fascinating mix of ancient (mainly) Hindu mythology and architecture. So difficult to believe it was built in modern times – 1939. I found the gardens themselves to be amazing and unforgettable. To be seen was a comprehensive range of stone animals from a rabbit to an elephant, including a bear, a camel, a duck, a monkey, a snake, a tiger and a turtle. Also, there were some small man-made caves with the entrances in the form of animals' mouths.

Just as dusk was coming, there was quite a fierce thunderstorm. As it happened, we were walking around Connaught Place at the time. It was most unusual to watch the storm as the darkness came.

Wednesday 19th. There was another thunderstorm this morning, and even at ten o'clock it was still very overcast. It looked as if there should be more rain to come, however, there was none.

Looking back at our twelve days in Delhi, I suppose that we have achieved some serious sightseeing and experienced some of the wonders of Delhi, both old and new. I hope it didn't sound too much like a travelogue by an ordinary sprog. I have tried to describe places which I actually visited, together with some individual experiences and also adding some facts and figures. There are many more attractions in Delhi to visit, but we were running short of time on our leave. So, as we depart the shores of – oops! – that does sound like an old-time Fitzpatrick travel film.

It was time to move on, in a southerly direction, 120 miles to be exact. The rail route would take us through Muttra (now Mathura) on the River Jumna. It was a mere thirty miles further on to the 'small' city called Agra, which would reach its forecast, a population of one and a half million by the 21st century!

Thursday 20th. The journey by train from Delhi took five hours and we arrived in Agra at 1.00 a.m. Why is it when we travelled by train, Ken and I always arrived at our destination during the night? We hired a tonga from the Agra Cantonment Junction to the City Leave Centre, where we went to bed almost immediately. By then it must have been almost two o'clock on the Friday morning.

After breakfast, we followed our usual pattern of Lahore and Delhi and hired bicycles, but this time also hired a guide. Now we were ready to explore Agra, a place which now enjoys no less than three UNESCO world heritage sites: Fatehpur Sikri, the Red Fort and that famous one, oh yes, the Taj Mahal, the primary reason for our visit to this area. We managed to investigate two out of the three, the finest we left until last.

Our expedition began in Agra with the Red Fort (Lal Qila, as at Delhi), situated on the banks of the Yamuna River. The history of this impressive site stretches back a thousand years.

From the Red Fort at Agra to a distant view of the Taj Mahal.

Built and renovated under diverse regimes throughout the centuries, this walled palatial city was the product of many different architects. It has been the home of many of the great Mughals – Babur, Humayun, Akbar, Jehanjir, Shah Jahan and Aurangzeb. In 1558, Shah Jahan's grandfather Akbar took over the fort, which was in a ruined condition, and rebuilt it, including the outer walls in red sandstone and the inner core with brick. There are two means of access, the Delhi Gate, and the one we entered, the Lahore Gate (also named the Amar Singh Gate) the main one for tourists. We found many sites and structures within the fort, reminiscent of the Fort at Delhi. Among them are Diwan-I-Am, Diwan-I-Khas. But the feature that mostly gripped my imagination like a band of steel, was an octagonal tower identified by the name of the Musamman Burj.

This was the site where Emperor Shah Jahan spent the last seven years of his life, imprisoned there by his own son, Aurangzeb. From the marbled balcony there was and still is, an excellent view of his beloved Taj Mahal, built by him, as a final resting place in homage to his favourite and cherished wife, Mumtaz Mahal. It was ironic that he was unable to cross the short distance of a mile and a half. If he had been allowed to go, he would have done it in style by either camel or elephant. Poignantly, when he died, he was taken to be buried there, next to his favourite wife for eternity. We are intending to make the brief journey by bicycle on his behalf, a camel ride that he was not allowed to do in his remaining years.

The Taj Mahal is considered to be the finest example of Mughal architecture and is one of the masterpieces of the world's heritage. Prince Khurram was 35 years old when he ascended the throne in 1627 and became Shah Jahan, which translates to 'King of the World'. It was built in memory of his favourite wife Arjumand Banu Begum, better known as Mumtaz-I-Mahal, from which is derived the name Taj Mahal. In 1631, he was grief-stricken when she died during the birth of their fourteenth child, Gauhara Begum. So, a birth led to the birth of the immortal Taj Mahal. Completed by 1653, it took twenty-two years and employed thousands of craftsmen and artisans. Passing through the huge gateway, we notice the illustration of calligraphy which reads: "O Soul, thou art at rest. Return to the Lord at peace with Him and He is at peace with you." As you emerge from the huge gateway, and the Taj appears, the most noticeable feature is the white domed mausoleum, which appears to be guarded by the four majestic minarets, one in each corner and supported by a marble platform 22 feet high. All this was surrounded by other buildings and the magnificent gardens.

We walked alongside the central waterway, lined mainly by tallish, slender cypress trees. In the centre of the gardens (Charbagh), about halfway between the gateway and tomb, there is a raised marble water tank (Al Hawd Al-Kawthar), reflecting the image of the Taj. We sat down there, with the Taj behind us. Little did we realize that almost forty-five years later, there would be someone sitting in the very same spot – Diana, Princess of Wales, looking very forlorn and lonely. It was during her royal tour of India, and the occasion virtually prophesied things to come – her divorce.

We continued on and aimed for the minarets, specifically to the one at the rear on the right-hand side. I believe that it is now forbidden for the general public to ascend any of them, but I may be wrong about that. However, in 1947, we were allowed to climb the 137-foot tower. Quite a climb, because there was no lift. Nevertheless, it was well worth it for a most unusual angle on the Taj, looking down on the huge dome tomb and back along the gardens all the way to the Gateway in the distance.

A unique angle for the general public from the top of the minaret, showing the gardens and the Gatehouse in the distance.

Our last glimpse of the majestic Taj Mahal from the bank of the River Jumna.

From the lofty heights of the minaret, we made our way down into the depths of the tomb to contemplate the centre of attention, the false sarcophagi of Mumtaz Mahal and Shah Jahan. Their actual graves are together, at a lower level. If the story of Richard Burton and Elizabeth Taylor was the love story of the twentieth century with his jewel of an engagement ring, then the narrative of Mumtaz Mahal and Shah Jahan must be the love story of all time, with the jewel of the Taj Mahal as the centrepiece.

Before we left, we viewed the Taj Mahal from outside the area with the River Jumna between. This river is almost nine hundred miles long, starting in the Himalayas and terminating its journey by joining the larger and religious River Ganges at Allahabad. At the world-famous site, I felt indeed in the presence of history – ancient history. And I believe that it is even more impressive by moonlight. But unfortunately, we will have to miss it. Our train leaves tonight and we must report back to camp tomorrow.

We had a brief walk to Agra town centre via Sadar Bazaar and acquired some connor. By then, it was time to hire a tonga to take us and our kit to Agra Cantonment Station. Our train was due to leave at twelve midnight.

Friday 21st. We finally arrived at Lahore at 8.30 p.m, just twenty-two hours after the start of our tonga ride the previous evening. And so ended our short visit to the capital of India. It was a most interesting time we had there, with some interesting experiences. But we had succeeded in achieving our target, the reason for visiting Delhi and Agra – the Taj Mahal.

Chapter 10
Third Day in Kashmir

Friday 1st August 1947. Starting the month of Partition, we are on our way to Gulmarg. A short journey for India, just a slight matter of thirty-two miles and a climb upwards of about 3500 feet. We were going to do it the easy way, or so we thought. Instead of the bus taking us all the way, it suddenly arrived at the terminus at a place called Tangmarg. There was a very good reason, that's where they ran out of road. But we were given a choice for the remainder of the journey. We could either hire a pony or proceed by Shank's pony. Considering neither Ken nor I had ever been on a pony, we obviously opted for the walk. In fact, it equated more to a climb, with Gulmarg being almost seven miles away and still 1300 feet above. But it was a very refreshing walk through the pine trees. One had to go slowly as the entire track was uphill and some places were quite steep, especially the last bit. However, being young, we could cope with it. Not that we had a choice. But it was ample reward when entering Gulmarg through the last of the gaps and we discovered a lush green meadow opening up before our eyes. Owing to the uneven terrain, it was forbidden for safety reasons to travel between the two places after dark! But of course, it was in daylight when we eventually arrived at Gulmarg. The name means 'meadow of flowers or roses', a delightful and suitable description. It is situated in a saucer-shaped valley girdled with poplar trees. An all-year-round resort, mainly for the winter months, with its heavy snowfall and the glorious ski runs totalling a distance of three miles. And in the summertime, it has trails in many directions, not just for walking, but also popular for riding ponies. The so-called Outer Circular Walk is a length of seven miles. When we were there, no cable car (or gondola) was running. One appeared, I believe, a few years later, and I would have loved to have experienced it. Particularly so, it is known as Asia's highest and longest, operating in two stages. Also, Gulmarg boasted being the highest golf course in the world at 2650 metres (8,690 feet) above sea level. It consisted of two 18-hole courses and a 9-hole one. Tournaments were arranged and were extensively covered in London newspapers.

After settling into our hotel here in Gulmarg, and despite our inexperience of pony riding, we agreed to undertake a recommended pony ride around the Outer Circular Route.

The road to Gulmarg.

A pony waiting for us outside our hotel.

At the start of the pony ride…

…and the Outer Circle Route with the sheer drop into space on the left.

For the entire journey this morning and even though Ken was with me, I truly missed the presence of Lotus. I was just going to mention it when I heard a familiar voice say, "Hello." I turned around and there she was in person. Without thinking, I blurted out, "I'm so glad to see you. I missed you."

She smiled and said, "I hope you don't mind."

"No, of course not. I'm delighted. Are you joining us on our pony adventure?"

"Of course, although I have done it before."

"Will you be coming to show us the way?"

"No, I wouldn't need to. Just follow the path around. Besides that, the ponies know the way better than I do."

We all looked at each other and laughed.

When the laughter diminished, Lotus exclaimed, "I must say I enjoyed reading your diary and seeing the photographs of Delhi and Agra. I thought it was very interesting and noticed that it covered most of the important places there."

"I'm glad you liked it," I commented, "but I'm certain that you know a lot more about the area."

"Yes, there were other places I could have mentioned, but you did very well in the time you both had there."

"Ken and I managed the most important one of all, the Taj Mahal. It is a most fascinating place, particularly with the love story behind it."

Lotus remarked, "I have always been fascinated with it."

Then she informed us, "We heard from Dad this morning that he will be coming on leave tomorrow."

"You must be happy about that. How long since you have seen him?"

"It must be a few months."

"You must miss not having him around."

"Yes, we do. But Mum wants to be at the hotel to run things and not travel around with Dad."

In the meantime, two more ponies appeared and we all three set off. At first it was very pleasant riding on level ground in the vicinity of the Gulmarg Bazaar. Then the jaunt became more hazardous. The mountain path on the right enjoyed a very acceptable slope upwards, but on the left it was a completely different matter. The path followed an abrupt descent into the valley. Looked like a drop of thousands of feet. And of course, the pony much preferred to be that side with my left foot hanging way over the edge. It was very disturbing. No matter how much I pulled the reins to the right, the beast insisted on keeping close to the brink. But as I said, we agreed to *undertake* a pony ride, an unfortunate word to choose. However, we survived and looking back on the event, I realised I had thoroughly enjoyed the entire experience, despite it being extremely unnerving.

After we dismounted back at our hotel, I started walking around Lotus and she turned with me.

"What are you doing?"

"Stand still," I commanded putting on a serious voice. She stood motionless, looking puzzled. After walking all around, I declared, "You are stunning from all angles. Oh, and you have a nice face." Then I reconsidered, shaking my head. "No. I'm wrong, you haven't a nice face!" To which she seemed surprised until I added with a smile, "No, it's a beautiful face."

She remarked, "You silly thing!" to which I replied immediately, "No, it's the absolute truth."

Later on, we were all relaxing in the bar with a drink at Nedou's Hotel, the leading hotel in Gulmarg, and felt that we had earned it after our pony experience! I was looking around the bar noticing the wooden flooring, the pillars, roof and the furniture. The hunting trophies on the walls including a tiger skin about six or seven feet long. The theme of blue and white tablecloths was very elegant. Through the window I could see the cup-shaped valley of Gulmarg. I also observed the uninterrupted view of the Apharwat Ridge which we intended to climb tomorrow, or at least partly.

Lotus broke into my contemplation of our surroundings. "This hotel was opened by a Michael Adam Nedou from Ragula in Croatia in 1888 and followed later on with his hotel in Srinagar." I commented, "A strange mixture, Croatia and Kashmir."

After a short pause, I asked Lotus, "Have you always lived in Kashmir?"

"Yes, my mum came to India with her parents in 1927. Her father was in the army, an officer serving in Delhi. My dad is from Delhi, old Delhi and he's also in the military. That's how my parents met. They were married in Delhi in 1930 and went on their honeymoon to Kashmir. They fell in love with the place as well as with each other and decided to stay. Dad stayed with the army and Mum bought the Srinagar Hotel. The hotel here in Gulmarg followed about two years later."

Then the three of us had an enjoyable chat about things in general, mainly about Gulmarg itself. As usual, Lotus came out with her usual account of facts. How she remembered them all I do not know. "Gulmarg is in its prime in both summer and winter. The resort has a very romantic and colourful history. It was believed to have been discovered by the last ruler of the independent state of Kashmir, a person by the name of Yusuf Shah Chak. It is thought that he with his wife Habba Khatoon camped here. The resort surely has something mystical and romantic about it. It is a very quiet and calm locality. Presently among the hotels of varying sizes, there are two containing one hundred rooms, a cinema, the famous Bazaar and hundreds of chalets. The Gulmarg Bazaar was famed throughout by the British gentry in India. Whatever one could not get in any part of the British Empire was available here. These included exotic perfumes, costumes, soaps and so on. They were specially imported from England to be stocked in the Bazaar."

"Quite an interesting and picturesque place is Gulmarg," I remarked, then continued, "Would you like to hear about our traditional but wacky Christmas on camp last year? Oh, do you know what wacky is?"

"Yes I do. It means crazy."

"What a clever girl! Now Ken and I can remember events last year and can back it up with some photographs as well."

A flashback to our 1946 Christmas on camp.

Wednesday 12th July 1946. A few months before Christmas we experienced a very severe dust storm this afternoon at 3.30pm. The hazy sky that had prevailed for several days suddenly turned brownish, the semi-darkness being like that before sunrise or after sunset. Many trees were uprooted, telephone and telegraph lines dislocated and some houses wrecked. In Mozang, a suburb of Lahore, an unfortunate five-year-old child was buried under the debris of a house. The dust storm was followed by a heavy shower which gave Lahore 1.66 inches of rain and a most welcome drop in temperature. On camp, soon after the wind started, it began raining. It fell almost horizontally, because from the very beginning of the storm the wind was blowing very hard. The trees shook violently. The tents were the first to go. Then the lights went out. We were all on the veranda watching. The rain was covering the whole ground. We kept hearing crashes, but at first could not see any roofs coming off. Then suddenly, the roof of 15 billet lifted right over and part of it went through the roof of 18 billet. A few bits came off 13 billet.

After about half an hour or so, the storm stopped and we surveyed the damage. Parts of the roof were off the cookhouse, a canteen and reading room. There were large pools of water between the billets and a lot of mud, bits of roofs, beams and boxes strewn all around the Domestic Camp. When we investigated the Technical Camp, there was damage to the Orderly Room, Workshops, the Armoury, Barrack Stores, 3, 5 and 7 Sheds. Also, one door had been blown in on each of Sheds 5 and 6.

It was overwhelming, and rumours were going around that the Unit would have to close down. But it seems the camp will survive and we will have the job to clear up. After the great storm and following the massive cleanup, on camp we all got back into the old work and play routine.

A few 'bits' came off the roof of number 9 billet.

The devastation at number 9 shed.

Several weeks had gone by. One morning I was fast asleep at about six o'clock. In my subconscious, I faintly heard what sounded like bells. I thought, no, it can't be, and dropped off to sleep again, only to be woken again shortly afterwards. Bells again, louder this time, sleigh bells. No, I thought again, it won't be sleigh bells in the heart of India, so I dozed off again. Suddenly the door of the billet burst open. I woke up with a start and heard a voice boom out, "Merry Christmas!" There was Santa standing in the doorway in full regalia and by now, I was awake enough to realise that the date was indeed the 25th of December 1946. I can always remember that episode but cannot for the life of me recollect if I received a present. I must have, because Santa was complete even with a sack! We never did find out who he really was. He may have flown down specially by an RAF plane from the North Pole. Or perhaps an airman or even an officer in disguise? That surprise was just the start.

We were issued with a menu of the bill of fare for the day. For breakfast we were served grapefruit, cornflakes, eggs and bacon, grilled tomatoes, fried bread, tea or coffee, bread and butter and marmalade. At dinner (lunchtime) we had the choice from roast chicken or pork, roast potatoes, creamed potatoes, cauliflower, peas, stuffing, bread sauce, apple sauce, brown sauce, Christmas pudding and brandy sauce, mince pies, coffee, cheese and biscuits, beer, minerals, nuts, apples, oranges and bananas, sweets, cigarettes and cigars.

In the afternoon, it got a bit surreal. A 'football' match was arranged. Not at all like the league games, back home in Blighty. The two teams competing were the officers and sergeants versus the men of 306 MU, but it was decided that feet would not be used, because the players would all be mounted on donkeys. They would bring into play mallets to hit the ball, so it was more like donkey polo. A Flying Officer was chosen to control the game as referee, but the masterstroke was that he had to perform his duties on a camel. Also, with it not being a normal game, he was *not* issued with the usual whistle. No, he had to keep the peace with a bugle. But the players never took notice of that and certainly the donkeys ignored the referee and bugle completely. In fact, the donkeys didn't co-operate very much either and they hardly moved at all. I seem to remember that remarkably, against all the odds, that at least one goal was scored. There was such a lot of inactivity with the donkeys. The players were very willing, but the donkeys refused to 'play the game'. The result was unknown or was declared a draw. All things considered, it was certainly a most unusual and extraordinary Christmas.

   I was never lucky enough to see elephants or tigers during my stay in India. I occasionally glimpsed camels from a distance, and I always thought they were an African animal. However, whilst the camel was on camp for the polo match, I thought it would be an opportunity to mount it for the experience and for a photograph for posterity. I got Ken ready with the camera. The camel was sitting down, which is the easiest way to get on board. It was a dromedary, that is the camel with just one hump. I climbed up and sat just in front of the hump. Now, the neck dips in front and you hang on somehow for dear life. I can't remember being told that when a camel stands up, it lifts its rear legs first. As a result, the passenger is thrown forward and I just managed to save myself from being thrown over the camel's head, very easily done. When it was standing, I discovered it was a long way up and precarious. I don't know how a rider can cross the desert on one! Nevertheless, I managed to stay on long enough for the photograph to be taken. Unfortunately, it was on one of those rolls of films which, inexplicably did not turn out. So much for posterity and nothing to show how I risked my life by sitting on the camel.

   In the evening there was a running buffet in the Canteen, most likely the leftovers from the dinner. The RAF cooks really 'went to town' on the Christmas cuisine. But the crcwning glory was the waiters, who were none other than our own officers, sergeants and corporals. A great finish to our festivities.

Pictorial record of the donkey match played at 306 MU Christmas 1946.

Our referee, complete with bugle.

A witch-doctor?   No, a linesman!

Just before a goal, I think.

After recounting our Christmas and storm on camp to Lotus, we chatted a while longer, until Ken left us about ten o'clock saying, "Another full day tomorrow sightseeing."

Again, the music was playing and I inevitably asked Lotus, "Would you like to have another little dance?"

"Yes, I would love to," she said and we got up to begin.

This time the song was 'I Can't Begin to Tell You', sung by Bing Crosby and Carmen Cavallaro. The composers were Mack Gordon and James V. Monaco. The words of the song came over loud and clear. Very thought-provoking words when we held each other closer until our lips touched. We were in a dream, at least I was. I wished for Lotus to feel the same. She suddenly broke into my thoughts by exclaiming, "Oh, I love dancing! It must be my Scottish blood on my Mum's side."

After dancing for a short while longer, it was hard for me to gather my thoughts as we went up to our rooms. Outside her room, we paused close together, our lips almost touching. Suddenly our lips met in a long, lingering kiss. And still hugging, we both said good night.

Chapter 11
Fourth Day in Kashmir

Saturday 2nd Aug. Today, we decided to 'hit the heights and reach for the sky'. Our target was to be to the south, overlooking Gulmarg. It is known as the Afarwat (or Apharwat) Ridge, rising to almost a further 6000 feet above the Gulmarg altitude. That would have been too ambitious, so we were aiming for a humbler objective, a mere 1300 feet above, at a place called Khilanmarg, which we were told would take about forty minutes. It sounded rather fast and I think it took us a lot longer, although I cannot remember exactly. We reached Khilanmarg just above the treeline.

The effort of the climb was well worth it. Our viewpoint above Gulmarg opened up a panorama stretching into the distance; a big proportion of it was cloud. Whilst taking in the amazing scene, I heard a voice at my side.

It was Lotus of course. "If you look in that direction," turning to my side, I saw her pointing straight ahead. She continued, "You can just see the summit of Nanga Parbat peeping through the clouds." I could make out a cone surrounded by cloud and realised that at 10,000 feet above sea level, I still had to look *up* to the mountain peak from a distance of eighty miles. Remarkable and so humbling. Human beings are so insignificant compared to nature all around us.

Lotus explained that Nanga Parbat is a giant of 26,666 feet, the ninth highest mountain in the world and soon to become the second highest in Pakistan. Another claim to fame is that the south face, recognized as the Rupal Face, is the tallest mountain face rising from its base, sheer for 15,000 feet. Its name translates to 'Naked Mountain', but it is also known as The Man Eater. It has a reputation of being a killer mountain, the deadliest in the first half of the twentieth century. It is now less so, but it is still a serious ascent. Climbers had been attempting to conquer it since 1895, but it was not finally achieved for several years yet, a long campaign and a worthy foe.

Whilst descending back to reality, I kept wondering if I had actually seen the giant Nanga Parbat. Not sure if I actually saw the snow-covered peak among its shroud of cloud, a summit that is just a mere 2400 feet short of the mighty Mount Everest itself. No need to climb it, just to see it was amazing.

Kashmir is situated in the western end of the mighty Himalayas and this mountain range extends for just over 1500 miles, finishing at Nepal and Tibet which are known as the roof of the world. Close to Mount Everest is the Rongbuk Glacier and Monastery with a view of the highest mountain in the world.

Apharwat Ridge, 14,403 feet; Khilanmarg, 10,000 feet (at the tree line); Gulmarg, 8,700 feet.

Some people have work to do, even in a holiday playground!

In the afternoon, we investigated the local bazaar (shopping area). Gulmarg Bazaar at the time was famous throughout the British population in India. It was stocked with lots of goodies. Whatever a shopper could not get in any part of the British Empire was available at this bazaar. These included exquisite perfumes, soaps, dresses, etc. These items were specially imported from England to be stocked in the bazaar.

It was only a brief look, and we did not have time to buy anything because we had left it late to get to our bus down at Tangmarg. As a result, we made our descent very fast, again not by pony. We found it easier, and faster of course, walking downhill. We caught the bus in good time, which guaranteed arriving back to Srinagar today.

Sadly, tomorrow is our last full day in Kashmir. But today there is still dinner back in Srinagar and also this evening, hopefully with the enchanting Lotus.

As it turned out, there was a surprise for me before we went into dinner. I don't know why, but I was passing the kitchen and paused in the doorway. The female chef preparing dinner looked very much like Lotus and I thought to myself it can't be. Her mother had already told me that Lotus doesn't help much in the hotel and certainly not with the cooking. But it *was* Lotus!

"Can I ask what you are doing?"

"I'm making the main course for the dinner tonight."

"Do you know how to?"

"Of course I do. The recipe has been given to me by my mum. It is for lamb masala and is an old family recipe handed down through generations." Moving closer to her, I studied her face.

"What are you looking at?"

"There is something on the tip of your nose. Oh, it's curry sauce. How did that get there?"

Before she could answer, I reached for a handy towel, then changed my mind and hung it back. And before she could move,

I immediately licked the sauce off her nose, commenting, "I knew you were sweet, but never realised you were spicy too."

Giving her little giggle, she said "Thank you", smiled and turned back to her cooking.

"Well, I'll leave you to it. I can see you are busy. I will look forward to tasting it later." With a smile I added, "Although I have already had a sample and I'm sure it will be great."

In the dining room at seven o'clock, we had Lotus serving us all our three courses and after the main course I said, "That was delicious! And after tasting it, all I can say is that you are an excellent cook. You will make someone a good wife!"

Was that a blush? I wondered. Then she said, "Oh. My dad is back on leave now and he asked if you would see him in the lounge after dinner. He said that Ken can be there as well."

"We'll be there. What is it about?"

"I do not know, but I will see you in there afterwards."

Ken and I entered the lounge puzzled why her dad wanted to see us. We had not long to wait before he arrived.

"Hello. You are Bob and Ken. I am very glad to meet you both."

"And we are very pleased to meet you," we both said almost at the same time.

"I had to meet you both to thank you so much for what you did for Lotus the other evening. She could have been in real trouble if you had not been there and reacted so swiftly."

I replied for both of us. "We were so lucky, perhaps fate, to be there at that moment and sort out her problem so very quickly."

"You must realise that I am very grateful, but there is something else I have to mention," he said with an awkward pause.

"You have been seeing Lotus a lot in the few days you have been here. In that short time, she does seem to have changed from a teenager into a young woman. Are you serious about her in such a brief time? Do you know she is only sixteen?"

"Yes, of course I do, and many young ones are childhood sweethearts and have a successful marriage, and I am attracted to her."

"I agree with that about childhood sweethearts, but there are other problems. Very soon, you will be returning to England almost halfway around the world and what chance will there be to meet again?"

I observed, "Destiny brought us together this week and could do so again."

"Here in India, we do believe in Fate or Kismet, but I would appreciate it, if you would consider it seriously."

"Yes, I will give it some thought."

"Theek Hai, OK. Enjoy the rest of your stay here in Kashmir."

With that, he left us. Not long after, Lotus walked in and joined us. We had a general chat as usual and after a short while, Lotus anxiously asked, "What did Dad say to you?"

"Oh. He mentioned to me that I will very soon be halfway around the world."

Looking down, all she said was, "Oh!"

We didn't really want to discuss or mention it. Ken commented, "It's difficult to know what to say."

Ken left us a while after to go upstairs. Lotus and I continued talking until we suddenly realised that someone had already put a record on. We looked at each other. "Yes?" I said, with a question in my voice.

"Yes please, Bob. I am ready for more practice," and she immediately stood up. I took her in my arms. We started moving slowly around the floor and I realised that she had called me by name for the first time.

Lotus commented, "Oh. I love dancing."

"You told me that last night."

"No, I mean dancing with you."

"Well. The feeling's mutual."

I realised the song playing was 'Till the End of Time' and singing the words was Perry Como. The composer was Ted Mossman. While we were dancing, I thought to myself, the more I see this girl, the more I realise that I could spend the rest of my life with her. But I'll not impart my thoughts to her. After all, we only met three days ago. I was interrupted in my thoughts by the record coming to an end and I went over to put on another. This time I chose a song called 'As Time Goes By', sung by Billie Holiday and which was composed by Herman Hupfeld for the famous movie *Casablanca* starring Humphrey Bogart and Ingrid Bergman.

Before the song had finished, we were kissing and sighing. After a couple more dances, we wended our way upstairs to our bedrooms, holding hands all the way. We paused at the door to her bedroom, kissed again and I thought that I would lighten the situation a bit.

I put on, or tried to, my best Shakespearean voice, "Ah. Parting is such sweet sorrow, but we must say goodnight."

My effort backfired a bit because Lotus exclaimed, "That sounds very musical. Did you just think of that yourself?"

"No, of course not. It was invented by Shakespeare."

"A friend of yours?"

"No again. It was written by the author Shakespeare."

"Does he live in England?"

"He wrote it about four hundred years ago!"

"Did he really?" she commented.

I nodded. We both laughed, kissed again and went to our rooms.

Chapter 12
Fifth Day in Kashmir

Sunday 3rd. After a night back in Srinagar and an early breakfast, Ken and I were ready for our last day of sightseeing. Yet again, I was surprised when Lotus appeared to guide for the day. She was in a simple, modest red dress with a high neckline and the hemline a few inches below her knees. She was wearing red sandals to match her dress. And, of course, she wore a necklace and Jhumka earrings, also with a touch of red. Wearing all the red, together with her long black hair, she looked very elegant, but also absolutely stunning.

After catching my breath, I managed to speak. "Ken and I thought that this morning we would visit a shrine at the top of a hill and spend the last afternoon at the lakes of Srinagar. How does that sound?"

"It sounds good. Let us get started."

We set off to tackle a hill 1100 feet above the city and valley, Mount Shankaracharya, overlooking Dal Lake.

I enjoyed helping Lotus up by holding her hand.

When we reached the top she said, "On this summit is situated a temple named Takht-I-Sulaiman", she said, "a shrine dedicated to the Lord Shiva. It is thought to be the oldest shrine in the Kashmir valley constructed in about 200 to 300 BC. Electricity was connected just 22 years ago."

Silently reflecting on the name Shankaracharya, it notably consists of six syllables, very rare in place names in India. Most of the names in the sub-continent are usually no more than four. However, diverting for a moment, a name that fascinates me the most is of only five syllables in length, Secunderabad. I have never been to the place because it is in southern India. But it is not the number of syllables that has always intrigued me. It is the way the word rolls off the tongue when you say it: Se-cun-der-a-bad. It is now known as Hyderabad, but not quite so 'rolling'. After that diversion of syllables, back to Shankaracharya. The hilltop is attained by approximately one hundred steps and paths, well worth the effort by offering splendid views down the valley and the mountains of the Pir Panjal range.

Our last afternoon in Kashmir was spent very pleasantly at the lakes, in fact with Lotus it was magic. The largest is Dal Lake, a very popular tourist area. It is about four miles long and two miles wide. The attraction is its serenity and solitude, so hard to believe it is in a city. Srinagar is the heart of Kashmir and in turn, Dal Lake is the heart of Srinagar.

The path to the summit of Mount Shankaracharya.

The lake is at its most beautiful when the lotus flowers bloom in July and August. Lotus, the flower not the girl, is known as Pamposh or Pummbuchh in the Kashmiri language and is a freshwater plant mainly grown in Southeast Asia. The flower is an inseparable essence of Kashmir and grows profusely in the lakes of Kashmir.

Adjoining Dal Lake are the floating gardens, known as 'Radh' in Kashmiri and which are one of the stranger things of the area. They are composed of matted vegetation and earth, cut away from the bottom and are towed to a convenient location where they are moored. Tomatoes, cucumbers and melons all grow amazingly well in these gardens. If you would look underneath, you could see that they do literally float on the surface. The shallowness of Dal Lake and its heavy growth of water weeds are probably the main reasons there are so few powered boats on the water. It wouldn't be so pleasant if there were speedboats rushing back and forth across its tranquil surface.

Two of the main attractions are the houseboats and shikaras. Of the former, there are many varieties moored around the lakes of Srinagar. They are literally floating hotels and are elegant and stately, comprising living quarters, lounges, dining rooms and of course, bedrooms. All furnished with carved wood furniture, together with embroidered rugs and fabrics. The large windows frame the glorious views alfresco, a masterpiece at the time of sunrise. If Ken and I had known about them beforehand, we would have booked one instead of a normal hotel. A missed opportunity! But if we had known, I would never have met Lotus. That is Kismet.

On the subject of the shikaras, they are an unusual, splendid, cultural symbol of Kashmir and are traditionally wooden boats of multiple sizes, particularly around the lakes of Srinagar. They are the Kashmiri version of the Venetian gondola. Unlike the poles used to propel the craft in Venice, they operate the shikara by spade-shaped oars. Shikaras are very versatile; commercially, they are likened to floating supermarkets, moving around laden with flowers, fruit, vegetables, groceries, pashminas and shawls. Then there are the workhorses, used for fishing or for harvesting weeds (usually for fodder). Some are even used as floating homes by poor people.

But their role to concern us is for transportation, i.e. as a taxi. They usually have space enough to seat up to six passengers, with the 'driver' seated at the rear like in the gondolas of Venice. We hired one to transport us to the smaller and arguably more beautiful Nagin Lake just over five miles away, connected to Dal Lake by a narrow waterway.

Dal Lake with Mount Shankaracharya towering above.

Nagin, or Nageen, is known as 'The Jewel in the Ring' and that comes from the many trees which encircle the small, deep blue lake. For the more adventurous, water skiing and fibreglass sailing boats are available, but we chose something much more sedate. Ken hired a rowing boat to potter around in. His home is near Portsmouth, so he would be used to boats. With the lake being a perfect place for swimming, I chose that.

I asked Lotus, "Do you swim?"

"I have never tried it."

My reply, "You should learn. It is important for all to know how to swim. I was a slow starter because I never attempted it at school. In fact, I only tried it for the very first time on camp in India. So, I now want to test out my newly acquired swimming skills in something bigger than the camp pool. When learning, I discovered that I preferred swimming under water to swimming on the surface, so I am going to try to reach the bottom of this lake."

"Are you sure you want to try that?" replied Lotus with concern, and continuing, "Nagin is about twenty feet deep."

"I feel brave. It is a challenge to attempt to reach the bottom. Wish me luck."

She smiled at me but seemed worried.

I plunged in, submerged immediately and discovered that it was a long way down, As I descended, I started disturbing mud near the target. Of course, I failed to reach my objective and consoled myself that if I had succeeded, it would have disturbed lots of mud. When I climbed out, Lotus greeted me with a kiss, half smiling, half crying, "You were a long time!" and then kissed me again.

"It did seem a long time and a long way down, but it was probably only a few seconds."

A brief time later we were sitting in silent reverence of the lake and the surrounding mountains. It had a serene and isolated ambiance, more so than the larger Dal Lake of 26 acres, which also has its own charm. We sat side by side, holding hands and looking at the surrounding backdrop of Nagin Lake. Gazing around, I had come to realise this was the last opportunity to behold the delightful scene. It was added to enormously by the presence of the girl in the red dress. The thought that Ken and I had to leave Kashmir early tomorrow morning, I deeply regretted.

However, today we still had time to go to the shops and observe the Kashmiris themselves. The women generally have such love for jewellery that their headgear, ears, necks and arms glisten with ornaments. The whole ensemble creates a most artistic and colourful effect. The men are mostly craftsmen working with papier-maché, gold, silver and wood.

The lotus flower is at its best in July and August.

Today, our last task (a very sad one) before returning to the hotel for dinner was to call at the bus office to confirm our return journey to Lower Topa tomorrow morning.

Just finishing dinner, Lotus came over to us and said, "With this being your last night in Kashmir, would you like a walk along the Boulevard at the side of Dal Lake. That is if Ken would not object to us leaving him on his own."

"Of course I wouldn't mind." Agreeing. "Enjoy the walk."

"Thank you Ken. It is appreciated," and turning to me she said, "Will you call for me upstairs when you have finished dinner?"

"Yes. OK, see you soon."

A few minutes later, I went upstairs to her room, knocked on her bedroom door. She called, "Come in."

I entered and when looking around the room, I discovered she was sitting on the edge of her bed. But I was astonished to behold that she was topless!

"What are you doing?" I asked, horrified. "You shouldn't do things like that. It could bring you all sorts of trouble." Then I turned and started leaving, "I'll wait for you outside your room," and with a smile I added, "But, still perfect! I forgive you."

By the time we met outside, she was ready for the walk and the matter was forgotten. Walking along holding hands by the side of the lake a little while later, I noticed it was getting dark, the mountains were disappearing into the dusk and the stars were starting to appear. Studying the stars, I commented, "I have often speculated about the twinkling stars. It is very difficult to decide in the darkness, if the lights are coming from a dwelling where people live on the mountainside or if it is the starlight coming all the way from outer space. It is very difficult to decide."

"I know what you mean. I have also wondered if people actually live in the twinkling lights that you see."

Strolling along hand in hand, I realised that we agreed in lots of things.

A few minutes later, we passed the place where we met on my first day and where Lotus had that nasty experience. She seemed to read my thoughts because she said, "Yes. It was a nasty experience, but I was so lucky that you and Ken were passing and intervened."

"If that wasn't fate, I don't know what is. Are you sure you feel no after-effects?"

"Definitely not," she confirmed firmly.

"I'm so very glad. That alone has made our trip to Kashmir extremely worthwhile. But with the added attraction of Kashmir itself."

Inevitably, later on we ended up in the lounge with Ken, talking of things in general, until Lotus asked us, "what were you both doing before you joined the Air Force?"

Ken told her that he was allowed to finish a course of tool making, "So that should get me a good job when I leave, and I will be marrying the girl that I am getting engaged to when I leave the Air Force."

"What did you do, Bob?" Lotus asked.

"Before I joined, I worked as a cinema projectionist. I enjoyed doing that, but what I would really like to do is to run my own travel agency. What would you like to do, Lotus?"

"I would like to work as a travel guide. Mm, that goes with a travel agency, does it not!"

After Ken had left us, we started our very last session of dancing. One of the songs was 'Night and Day', composed by Cole Porter and sung by a famous dancer Fred Astaire. My thoughts were with Lotus all the time, but I still never expressed them out loud to her. Then the last dance came very quickly, 'We'll Meet Again', sung by the famous Forces Sweetheart of World War Two, Vera Lynn.

The recording was playing out, our last dance, but I don't believe I heard it very much. I was thinking about only knowing her the three days and before I could stop myself, I blurted out, "I can't imagine where or when we will meet again." I could have kicked myself for saying it, but her reaction was to remain extremely silent with no reaction at all. Not long after that, we strolled upstairs embracing as we went. She remained quiet. When we reached the landing, we shared a lingering kiss.

"Goodnight, sweetheart," I sighed.

"Goodnight to you too, darling," said Lotus, giving me a very brief kiss and adding, "I will watch you leave in the morning. I will be very sad, but I don't want to miss seeing you both leave."

Dal Lake with Hari Parbat Fort outlined at eventide.

This painting of Srinagar is by the author.

Aspects of this painting of Srinagar, Kashmir:

1) The mountains of the mighty Himalayas.
2) The enchanting lakes of Dal and Nagin.
3) Lotus flowers floating on the lakes.
4) A shikara, the Kashmiri version of the gondola.
5) The tall and stately trees – chenar, deodar and poplar.

Although not shown in the painting, the gardens are also a great attraction in Srinagar.

KASHMIR

"If there is paradise on earth, this is it." – Mughal Emperor Baber.

"To call Kashmir just a piece of heaven on earth. It is in fact… the sum total of many heavens." – Swami Abhedanada

Chapter 13
Back to Lower Topa

Monday 4th. Rising very early today, at 5.30 to catch our bus back to Lower Topa. Lotus came with us to the departure point. We arrived there after a hurried breakfast with just 15 minutes to spare.

"I have to say that it has been a marvellous experience these last five days," I said. "In fact, I'm sure I will remember it for the rest of my life."

"Yes, just unforgettable," Ken added.

"All the amazing things," I said, turning to Lotus, "Particularly the face I will never forget."

And we then all became silent and had nothing to say, lost for words, until the bus driver beckoned to us to come aboard.

Lotus said quietly, "I too will never forget it."

I raised both my hands, gently caressing her cheeks and chin. Then we kissed goodbye.

"I'll write to you tomorrow," I promised. "It will be too late tonight."

We started turning towards the bus, but before I had hardly moved Lotus rushed to me and put her arms around me and cried, "Bobee, do not go!"

"But I have to report to my camp by 23.59 hours," I replied and in explanation I added, "That is before midnight tonight. Your father in the military will understand that it is important to report on time."

I noticed Lotus had tears in her eyes as we kissed goodbye again. I felt very sad as I followed Ken on board. We all waved until the bus turned a corner out of sight of Lotus, the absolutely enchanting Lotus.

Immediately, I was reflecting on the last five days and I must have had a confused look on my face, because Ken asked me, "What's the matter?"

"What have I done? WHAT HAVE I DONE?"

"What do you mean?"

"We'll soon be going nearly halfway round the world. How can I possibly meet Lotus again? I have deceived her and misled her."

"You are thinking too much about what her father said the other night."

"How can I hope to return all this way to her and Kashmir when I leave the Air Force?"

"There is just no answer to that." We both said it together.

The journey from Srinagar and Lotus will take at least six hours, but I cannot truthfully say that I remember any of the drive back to camp in the Murree Hills. Nevertheless, the bus must have retraced the same route in reverse, I made a mental recap. Pattan, Baramula, Uri, Lal Put Bridge, Chakothi, Garhi, Domel, Kohala and finally our temporary Hill Station at Lower Topa. My heart and mind must have been still back in Srinagar, still imagining all the amazing wonders which we had experienced, the Vale of Kashmir, Shalimar, Hari Parbat Fort, Tangmarg, Gulmarg, the pony on the Outer Circular path, Khilanmarg, Nanga Parbat, Shankaracharya, the craftsmen, the bejewelled ladies, Dal Lake, the Floating Gardens, the shikara ride and the swim in Nagin Lake. And above all, the beautiful Lotus, my own lotus flower of Kashmir. All of which merged to make an everlasting impression.

I returned to my unhappy thoughts on my way back to Camp from Kashmir and Lotus. But it might console me by trying to remember my pleasant experiences at Lower Topa last year. There was an unwritten(?) regulation that all serving personnel stationed in the hot plains of the summer, had to have a compulsory break of three weeks in the hills to cool off, to the foothills of the Himalayan Mountains.

June 1946. There was a string of Hill Stations along the foothills of the Himalayas and no doubt still are, such as Simla, now known as Shimla. The resort was named after Shyamala Devi, a re-incarnation of the Hindi God Kali. Simla was declared the summer capital by the British, who nicknamed it 'Queen of the Hills'.

There was also Naini Tal. Founded by the British in 1841, it is set around a pear-shaped lake and is two miles in circumference. This lake is said to be one of the emerald eyes of Shiva's wife, Sati.

Another important hill station is Darjeeling, noted for various things. First, it is famous for its tea industry Second, for the Darjeeling/Himalayan Railway, also a UNESCO heritage site and not lastly for being in the proximity of Mount Everest. In the nineties, there was a marathon started in the area – the 'Mt. Everest Challenge Marathon'. Quite a challenge! Runners had to negotiate trails which varied in altitude from 11815 feet to 10900 and back to 11815. It has been called 'The World's Most Beautiful Marathon', because the five highest mountains on earth can be seen at all times. It may be the most beautiful, but certainly wouldn't be the easiest at those heights. Unfortunately, as I thought at the time, my Hill Station destination was none of these. It was to be further to the north at a place called Lower Topa, situated in the Murree Hills, towards Kashmir.

Tuesday 11th June 1946. My name appears in the SROs (Station Routine Orders) hill party list and we are due to leave camp on Friday. I kept a diary.

Friday 14th. At 16.45, we are told that the train will be four hours late, so we all decide to wait some of the time at camp. A few of us passed the time in the canteen having some connor (something to eat) and playing billiards.

After a gharrie (lorry) ride to the railway station in the semi-military part of the city at Lahore Cantonment (I believe pronounced Cantoonment) the train finally left at 23.05, almost Saturday! It was a military train and about a quarter of a mile long. I was in a compartment for four people and we were all asleep just about an hour later.

Saturday 15th. We were woken up suddenly, when the train clattered through a town called Lalamusa and went to sleep soon after until 06.45. The train was pulling into the city of Jhelum, after crossing the River Jhelum, one of the five big rivers of the Punjab Province. A railway man at the station said it was 65 miles to Rawalpindi and will take about four hours, less than 20 miles an hour, probably because of the length of the train. We found out while stationary that not only were there lads from our camp, but also from other camps including 307MU, an RAF camp situated much nearer Lahore than we were. A char wallah brought tea to all the carriages. We left Jhelum at 08.20 and just after leaving, got very excited. We had caught our first glimpse of the mighty, vast, impressive Himalayas. But in fact, what we could see were only the foothills. Nevertheless, it made me think of all the experiences to come. Despite this anticipation, when we stopped at a place called Domeli, I managed to have breakfast of tinned meat, beans, bread and butter and char. As we progress further, the hills get higher and the valleys deeper. At 10.30, we are stationary at a small town called Sohawa and we are told by a flight sergeant that the train should arrive at Rawalpindi by 14.30. And surprise, surprise, that was exactly the time we pulled into the station. We had a sandwich and char, while talking to another Hill Party group and discussing the journey. Rawalpindi is the end of the railway line, as far as we were concerned. It runs on for another one hundred miles to Peshawar, a city originally established as far back as the sixteenth century during the Mughal Dynasty. Throughout most of Peshawar's turbulent history, it was one of the main trading centres on the ancient Silk Road. The city is named from the Persian, translating as 'the place at the frontier'. And in fact, to the west just about thirty or forty miles past Peshawar, is the border with Afghanistan at the famed Khyber Pass.

However, from the station at Rawalpindi we are to travel in an easterly direction by road to the Hill Station in the Murree Hills in RAF gharries (lorries). No more than ten miles into our road journey, we passed through an area that is part of the Indus Valley and could also be known as the crossroads between the Punjab and the North-West Frontier. It is historically one of the earliest settlements of ancient civilisation in the world. No sign of a city, but in the 1960s a city was built, destined to be the new capital of Pakistan and taking over from Karachi, the vast and still young city of Islamabad. It is hard to believe that when we passed through the area in 1946, there was not the least sign of this large capital city of the future.

After passing the site of the forthcoming capital of Pakistan, the last part of the trip by road was something I shall never forget. It took a total of two hours 15 minutes. Starting at Rawalpindi at 1900 feet above sea level and ending at the height of 6800 feet at our destination, a total climb of almost 5000 feet in the 39 miles. Luckily, we stopped about halfway for a mug of char at Saligram Bridge and we needed the break to catch our breath. It was an unbelievable experience, roads on the sides of high hills with valleys of thousands (it seemed) of feet just a few inches from the gharrie's wheels. Sharp corners, which meant a fall of thousands of feet, if the turn was a foot or two out! It was an exciting journey, but after all the bends, slopes, drops, etc., we were relieved to reach our destination, No.1 Hill Station, Lower Topa, which has all the amenities of 306MU. The camp is built on the side of a mountain, with deep valleys not far from the billets and other buildings. Not the place for sleepwalkers! Then there are the mountains towering above the camp. Yes, they were mountains, even though locally they were called hills. Hills more than double the height of those in Snowdonia, the highest in the southern part of Britain. What a setting with mature pine forests, amidst the scenic area known as the Murree Hills. The atmosphere was exhilarating, heady and invigorating. A unique experience looking down at the drifting cloud formations and sometimes they were at eye level. When darkness arrives in these mountains, it is a weird and wonderful sensation to look up into the sky and see a light shining there, it might *not* be a star or planet, but in actuality it could be someone's home. Amazing, but that comes of always experiencing life on the Plains (no hills or mountains) at home in my short life. It was a new experience for me to be among mountains. It was the start of my love for mountain scenery, mainly I might add, to look at and not to climb!

Saligram Bridge where we stopped for a break.

Winding ways.

Panoramic view of Lower Topa. The main road across the middle: left to Rawalpindi, right to Kashmir.

Lower Topa Camp itself was established by the British during their rule of the Indian Sub-continent and since then has been the site of a Pakistan Air Force Camp and also a public boarding school run on British public school lines.

An unexpected feature on camp is the football field which overhangs 'space', right on the edge of a steep drop. Many a football must have disappeared, never to have been seen again. But luckily, we never heard of any players doing the same.

The town of Murree is the largest in the area and is four miles by road around the valley. But just two miles uphill along the road from the guard room of the camp is the village of Jhika Gali or Jeeka Gali, a cute little place at a junction of roads. This small village contains about twenty shops, two or three cafes including Robert's Cafe and one cinema, the Lansdowne. One of the shops was a bookshop and I recall buying a book there. The book was a Webster's Dictionary; it gave me good service, until it fell to pieces many years later. Webster's Dictionary was mentioned in a song made famous by Bing Crosby and Bob Hope in the movie *Road to Morocco,* with a pun on the words 'Morocco bound'. Sad to say, my copy was not Morocco bound, but just covered by cardboard. It would have lasted many more years, if it *had* been bound in leather! Just the same, it was precious to me, so I made sure it didn't go astray, by putting my address on the fly leaf as follows: name, rank, 306 Maintenance Unit, Harbanspura, Lahore, Punjab, India, Asia, World, Universe! My dictionary was Blighty bound and I kept it for well over fifty years. By then, the pages were yellowing and becoming loose. It was also flaking off at the edges, so I gave it a decent send off after all the years of service by placing it gently into the green bin, for recycling. Hopefully to reappear later as a brand new and shiny book, perhaps reincarnated as a dictionary.

The football field on the edge of the world.

Close-up of winding way from Jhika Gali to camp.

This winding road from Jhika Gali back to camp shows only half the story. On the right-hand side, it doesn't reveal the sheer drop into the valley. From Jhika Gali, it is a two-mile walk or gharrie ride downhill back to camp and a few times we hired bikes to ride back, quite a hair-raising ride. No pedalling is needed, a very twisty road with the right-hand side of the road disappearing down into the valley. But if you went over the edge, there is no danger of ending up at the valley bottom. No, the descent would be stopped long before, by all the trees on the steep slope. What happened to all the bikes on this one-way traffic? The chicos came specially from the village to reclaim them and had to cycle back up the hill with them, to return them to the rental shop.

The town of Murree was reputed to be 7000 feet above sea level, but they have since discovered it is more like 7500 feet. The name derives from Marhi, meaning high place, aptly named! The heart of the town adheres to the steep hillside. As in Lahore, the main street is called the Mall.

There was a gharrie service available at times for the journey of four miles between camp and Murree town via Jhika Gali. There was also the local bus service, but it was a hair-raising event. The local drivers travelled at 30 mph round the sharp bends and missing the edge by a foot or two. There are lots of steep hillsides in the Murree Hills. The local transport at the time was known as PMT – Pindi Murree Transport.

The climate here must be similar to back in Southern England, because fruits like cherries, raspberries and strawberries thrive here too.

It seemed to me that Murree felt like the very big brother of Jhika Gali village and of course with a lot more facilities. For instance, there is a big purpose-built Post Office erected by the British to cover mail service to the troops. It still remains to this day as a main hub of hill station activity. The Holy Trinity

Church was built and consecrated in 1857, the same year as the Indian Mutiny. The main street is known as the Mall and it goes without saying that there are only shops on one side, because on the other side is the inevitable drop to the deep valley.

There was a serviceman's club called the Uniacke Services Club, which organised dances and where the forces could stay for about five shillings (25p) a day. Bring those days and prices back. Somehow, I don't think they will ever return. Also, there was Sandes Home, a hostel which was additionally used for social gatherings. A popular meeting place was the Lontitt Café and there was a choice of two cinemas, doubling the number in our local village of Jhika Gali. During my first visit to the town, I bought a pair of chaplis (sandals).

Murree has expanded since 1947 at a greater rate than that which its infrastructure can sustain. Securing services like water and electricity are a constant challenge, owing to the mountainous landscape.

Back on camp, I had decided to take a War Education Certificate Examination, entirely voluntary. Possibly of not much use in civvy street, but it helped to pass the time. And there was a total of five keen applicants. It was to be held at Upper Topa, four miles from camp, again via Jhika Gali, but in the opposite direction of Murree from the village. All five of us decided to take a short cut up the mountainside and thereby reducing the distance to a mile or so. In the morning, we took two subjects, English and maths, and after some connor in the canteen at lunchtime, we took general knowledge in the afternoon. Coming down, all five of us lost our way on the mountainside. Jim and I climbed a small hill to try to catch a glimpse of Lower Topa, to enable us to get our bearings. We could see it, but there was no visible path, because the mountainside was too hilly and had many trees and large rocks on the steep slope. The other three decided to go back to Upper Topa and ring up the MT (motor transport) section back at Lower Topa for a gharrie. On the other hand, Jim and I decided to risk carrying on. From our observation hill, we knew the general direction of our camp, so we kept to the route as much as possible. With relief, we soon located the path that we went up on. It's too big a place to be lost in the Himalayas, even if it is only in the foothills. The remainder of the party arrived back about half an hour later than us, after also walking down. I don't know what happened to their transport.

Sunday 23rd June 1946. There was a fierce thunderstorm this afternoon with very heavy monsoon rain. It lasted almost an hour. Immediately after rain or a storm in the mountains there is a new feeling in the atmosphere. The quality of the air changes. With the menacing clouds still hugging the mountains, usually at your level or sometimes above, the air feels both cool and warm at the same time.

Thursday 27th. This evening some lads, including myself, held an impromptu tune-guessing competition and we also discussed which ones were harder to sing. We all agreed that one of the popular songs of the day, 'I'll get by (As long as I have you)' was more difficult to sing, because when the singer reaches the second 'I', the scale goes up considerably. We all had trouble with that.

Saturday 29th. Woke up to heavy rain. After it cleared a bit, we could see right down to the plains, which must have been around 40 miles away, in the Rawalpindi direction. It was a marvellous extensive view.

Monday 1st July. Early this morning, atom bombs were dropped in the Pacific Ocean on Bikini Atoll and on the fleet. It was part of a series of tests, named Operation Crossroads and was intended to study the effects on warships, equipment and material.

Tuesday 2nd. The town of Murree was out of bounds

yesterday but is now all clear. We never heard why, but it has possibly to do with the future partition of the sub-continent within the next two years.

Wednesday 3rd. Listened to the wireless this morning and heard just the end of a broadcast by Geraldo and his Orchestra. Then a programme called *Introducing Carole Carr* started at 11.15 and she was singing 'I can't begin to tell you'. She followed that with what must have been a new one, 'I'm glad I waited for you'. Over the last few days, I exposed a roll of film, but was disappointed today to find out that none of the photos turned out.

Thursday 4th. Paddy came to Lower Topa today on two weeks' sick leave from our camp at Lahore. He told us about the unpleasant heatwave endured in that area, during which the temperature reached about 115F. He told us that many inhabitants in the city and three RAF personnel have died of heatstroke. Very upsetting. He also told us that a fire has damaged our cinema. Other news that he gave us was that up to number 46 Demob group in most trades will be out by September. I still have a long way to go yet, being number 69. I received a letter today from home that took five and a half months to reach me. It was posted a week after I left home for Heaton Park. It was sent on to North Weald and was posted via 1588 Draft to 306MU and was re-directed to Lower Topa, finally to receive it on parade.

Friday 5th. No money left! So, I sold my cigarette ration and the chaplis (sandals) which I had bought earlier in Murree. I got 7 rupees (just over 50p!) for them. A notice has appeared in the dining hall today and our hill party are due to be leaving Lower Topa at 8.30 on Sunday.

Saturday 6th. The last full day today. I went to Jhika Gali in the morning on the RAF gharrie, took some snaps of the district and had an exciting ride back to camp on a bicycle. In the afternoon, I heard Harry Roy and his Band on Radio SEAC Ceylon.

Amongst other tunes they played were 'Bombshell from Brooklyn' and 'Gertie from Bizerte'.

In the evening, I went for the last visit to Jhika Gali and again cycled back to camp. This time it was particularly thrilling, because it was dark and I had a dynamo working to light the way. It seemed that I was moving faster than the light when I came to the corners.

Sunday 7th. We were supposed to have left at 10.30, but our departure was delayed until after tiffin (lunch). None of us complained, because it meant that we spent a little longer in the hills. Eventually we left at 13.30, arriving at Rawalpindi Station by 15.00 hours, after another gamble with the mountain roads. I wondered if we were getting used to it. No, not really. However, the journey down was wizard. There were five of us sitting on our kit on the back of the gharrie. We talked and sang all the way to the station. We were doled out 'connor' at a mixed rest camp by the station, before we boarded our train, which left at 22.30. All of us retired almost as soon as the train started. Even young lads get tired.

Monday 8th. I woke up at 05.30. The train was standing in Jhelum Station and I managed to keep awake long enough to see the bridge and River Jhelum. Our breakfast was at 08.30, a packet of K rations and a cup of char each. The K Rations were not loved very much, but they had their uses. They came in a 'carry-size' lightweight carton and contained 3000 calories. They were designed to pack into the soldier's kitbag and to be consumed when no other food is available, i.e. on long journeys (as in our case) and also for men being sent into combat. There were three sections in each pack, for breakfast, dinner and supper. They were designed to be eaten in the named order, but not all were consumed in this manner. Each section contained four cigarettes, probably voted the best part! The contents varied accordingly and consisted mainly of chopped ham and egg, biscuits, cheese, chocolate, milk powder, malted milk, sugar tablets, chewing gum and a tablet to be crumbled up in boiling water.

We reached Lahore at 12.15 and a gharrie was waiting for us. We got back to camp in time for connor, ending the most exciting holiday that I have ever had. It was a truly remarkable experience, living in the foothills of the mighty Himalayas for nearly four weeks, in among the sky-scraping mountains.

And so ended my first visit in June 1946 to Lower Topa. I felt slightly better after the silent reminiscing, but I was still unhappy and depressed about leaving Lotus and Kashmir.

Chapter 14
The sun rises on Partition

Tuesday 5th August. My first day back from Kashmir. I write a letter to Lotus as promised.

"Only just one day has passed since I left you at Srinagar and already, I miss you so much." But I never mentioned that we will soon be about seven thousand miles apart, even though at the moment we are separated by a mere one hundred and fifty miles.

The clock is ticking unremittingly towards Partition of the sub-continent. Our time at Lower Topa should be at an end. We arrived here just about four weeks ago and our stay at the Hill Station would in normal times be completed. By now, we should be on our way back to camp at Allahabad. But this isn't normal times on the sub-continent. If we are to be out of India by the 15th, we have a long way to travel until then, via our camp at Allahabad.

Saturday 9th. Received a reply from Lotus, part of which was: "You have gone away and my heart went with you." We then exchanged letters regularly in the ensuing weeks, although deliveries were disrupted somewhat due to the impending Partition.

Tuesday 12th. Lower Topa. We are still here, and it is now obvious that we are not leaving India by the 15th. So, more sightseeing, to a viewpoint of the Murree Hills, Monkey Hill (Dheer Ladhal), and such a good vantage point at 6900 feet high, that it claims having an old fire lookout tower. It overlooks a wide, undulating area of pine forests. Fire can be a hazard in this kind of region. The 'precipice' nearby was another popular hill to climb.

Wednesday 13th. Making the most of our remaining time here in India. This time we went on a trip to Bhurban, a minor resort, but with fine views overlooking the town of Murree and across the River Jhelum into Kashmir with even a view of the mighty Nanga Parbat on a clear day. Unfortunately, we picked a day when it was completely in cloud. No bonus of a final glimpse before leaving India. We went on guard duty today but it was called off at midnight.

Thursday 14th. The first of two days of a momentous occasion in Asian history, in fact in world history. Lord Louis Mountbatten came to India back in March, to attempt a superhuman task in record time. The structure of Partition involved so many complicated issues: religion, politics, geography and culture. Then there were all the provinces, Princely States and Maharajahs to take into account. Concerning the Princely States (and there were 625 of them), the rulers were given a choice to freely accede to either India or Pakistan or to remain independent. For example, Kashmir. The current Maharajah at the time was a Hindu and so chose to join India, which has most unfortunately led to bitter conflict between the two countries ever since. Pakistan claimed a section of it, Azad (Free) Kashmir, creating an extremely delicate situation.

A particularly huge, complex and thorny problem was sorting out the partition line between the two countries, stretching no less than 1800 miles. Particularly the border in the Punjab near Lahore and Amritsar. Which side of the border should they end up? It was finally decided that it would be about halfway between Lahore Pakistan and Amritsar India on the Grand Trunk Road at a place called Wagah, which for many years, was to be the only road crossing between India and Pakistan. This village was split in two by the Partition, the west side to Pakistan and the east to India. Sometimes it has been known as the 'Berlin Wall' of Asia. The location now gives its name to an extremely strange but entertaining ceremony every evening at sundown. There are mixed feelings about it. Some people treat it as an outing with picnics, etc., whilst others view it as enhancing the atmosphere of hatred. Whatever the opinion, it is certainly a colourful ritual. Crack troops from both countries marching in perfect drill, each on their own side of the border and showing their flag with pride.

The boundary as a whole, was known as the Radcliffe Line, drawn up by Sir Cyril Radcliffe, the Chairman of the Boundary Committee. With a population of ninety million, Pakistan celebrated independence on this day, 14th August, in the capital of the new state, Karachi.

The event was attended by Mohammed Ali Jinnah, the first Governor General and known as 'The Great Leader' (Quaid-I-Azad). Also present was Liquat Ali Khan, the first prime minister. Unfortunately, neither survived more than a very few years, but at least they saw their ambition fulfilled. They also witnessed Pakistan become a new nation member of the United Nations just over a month later. With Partition, Pakistan was divided into two sections, east and west, with 1000 miles of India between. But since 1971, the eastern section broke away and became recognised as a separate state, Bangladesh.

The birth of a nation, illuminated for the occasion.

Friday 15th August. India observes their Independence today. Jawaharlal Nehru (India's first prime minister) raised the Indian tri-colour flag above the ramparts at the Red Fort in Delhi. The country had been a member of the UN since 1945.

Mohandas Karamchand Gandhi, otherwise known as Mahatma Gandhi, a charismatic and amazing character, was one of the most pivotal in bringing about Partition. During a visit to Srinagar, it was his belief that the future of Kashmir should be decided by the will of the Kashmiris. He also said that all men were created equal, and it cost him his life when only five months later he was assassinated by a member of his own Hindu faith. He appeared as one of the most outstanding, outspoken and truthful human beings of the twentieth century.

The Partition of the sub-continent was an exceptional event of the twentieth century, but the repercussions were catastrophic on the populace. There was an estimate of one million killed on all sides and there were between ten and twenty million refugees. It was one of the largest and most rapid population transfers in history. In the exodus, they travelled on foot and in bullock carts, crammed onto lorries, clinging on to the roofs and sides of trains, anything to get them away. The Hindus were fleeing from the newly formed Muslim country of Pakistan, and the Muslims in the reverse direction, with the Sikhs involved in the middle. It was an utter human tragedy for all sides.

There were many reports of the actual figures and one reported a total of 17.9 million movements and only 14.5 arriving, suggesting that three to four million were missing. There was massive slaughter on all sides. All were victims and all were guilty of attacks. There was no one group to blame.

No words are needed.

Celebrations in the town of Murree.

To mar the celebrations, dreadful humanitarian things were happening. It is estimated that one million were killed, with ten to twenty million displaced. And many colleges, temples, gurdwaras, military barracks and many other forms of shelter were turned into refugee camps. The Purana Qila in Delhi was turned into a huge refugee camp for some fortunate survivors.

There were attacks on refugee trains, reminiscent of the hold-ups in the American Wild West, but with a more sinister motive. They were highly organised affairs. These trains generally carried three to four thousand refugees, inadequately accompanied by small escorts for protection. Death tolls sometimes reached two to three thousand, an extremely high price. As a horrific example, it was shocking when a trainload of Hindus and Sikhs fleeing from the Punjab pulled into Amritsar Station across the Indian border. It was discovered that the majority of them had been massacred. There were bodies all over the carriages, some leaning out of the windows. It was just too dangerous to travel by train and no one knew when it would be safe. So, we were stranded up here with millions of others around India and Pakistan.

Adding to all of the confusion, the vast majority of the public didn't recognise the perpetrators. It was widely reported that the local population harboured no ill feelings towards the other religions. They did not turn against each other in the name of religion but offered protection to each other. Up to the mid-1940s, Hindus, Muslims, Sikhs, Jains, Buddhists, Christians, Parsis, Jews and others had been existing peacefully for at least a couple of centuries in the region across South Asia. Neighbours did not recognise those committing murder, rape and pillage and believed them to be outsiders.

It was astonishing in the midst of all this that the British, both service personnel and civilians it seemed, were not caught up in this turmoil. It was not the case almost a hundred years before, during the Indian Mutiny (or War of Independence) when there was savagery on both sides. Also, going back almost two hundred years, 20th June 1756 to be precise, there was the notorious episode known as 'The Black Hole of Calcutta' and over the years, there has been controversy whether it was fact or fiction. It seems the troops of the Nawab of Bengal (Siraj ud-Daulah) captured Fort William on the eastern banks of the Hooghly River. They imprisoned a total of 146 British and Anglo-Indian soldiers and civilians. It was reputed they were held in a dungeon, not intended for more than two or three men at one time. There were only two windows and thick iron bars prevented much-needed ventilation in the cell They were held in there all the night, and by morning, most of the prisoners had died from heatstroke, suffocation or trampling. 123 of them had died during the night.

However, and fortunately for the Brits, the previous turbulent history of the country was not repeated in 1947. The presence of the British in India spanned 335 years and commenced in the year 1612 when the East India Company was established. Their influence continued until just after the Mutiny in 1858 and then it was the period of the British Raj until Partition.

Tuesday 26th. We are still here at the Hill Station. Eleven days have elapsed since Partition. We have been informed that service personnel and civilian workers are now prohibited from travelling by train. We can say that we are now stranded up here, but that is no hardship, an extended stay in the hills. But you had to feel sympathy for the general population.

To try to cheer ourselves up, we decided to have a get-together and have a singsong. It led to a discussion about music and songs. One thing I can remember discussing was a song that was popular during World War II. It was called 'I'll Get By' and all agreed that it was a hard song to sing. At the start of the song, the scale suddenly went up high and we struggled to reach the note. No budding Frank Sinatras there.

Friday 29th. Today, the hill party from RAF Palam at Delhi left to return to their camp. Is our departure also imminent? Guard duty started again today.

Sunday 31st. Curfew at Murree, so the trouble still carries on, although I must say that here at Lower Topa we are isolated from any rioting or unrest. Nor do we usually hear about any, when on camp. It is said that 'no news is good news', but in the current situation, I'm not so sure.

Wednesday 3rd September. On guard duty tonight. Many are excused for various reasons. For those not exempt, like myself, the duty has been coming around every three nights.

Thursday 4th. By now, our hill party have been here for almost two months, double the length of the normal stay. Surely, we will be due to leave at any time now, so we are all waiting to be back at Allahabad before getting our hair cut. Our hair does appear to be longer than regulations allow. On parade this morning, the NCO in charge went along the ranks and said, "You were all issued with rifles," in a normal voice. Then he went round to inspect our backs and slowly came round to face us again. He scrutinised us for a few seconds, then with a voice increasing in volume, repeated, "You were all issued with rifles," then marching slowly up and down in front of the parade, he snarled, "You should have been issued with violins," then shouted, "Get your hair cut!". The barber on camp did a roaring trade that day.

For the last few weeks, Lotus and I had been corresponding through Lower Topa, but gradually the mail kept taking longer and longer. In fact, we heard that the route our bus took through to Kashmir has now closed down, owing to the problems during the Partition period. Only local families were allowed through Border Control. The bus company was not only for carrying passengers, but was also the official mail carrier, which has now ceased to exist. The result was for all post to be diverted via

Jammu and Delhi. This detour was more than a thousand miles further, so mail in transit would take much longer than normal to deliver.

Friday 5th. All guard duty has been cancelled. We have finally heard that we are to leave on the ninth. How ironic. We all had our haircuts yesterday!

Very sad, our last visit to Murree today. But before we did that, I had a very important matter to deal with, a letter to Lotus immediately to let her know the full address of the camp I am very soon being transferred to.

Saturday 6th. More sadness! We said our goodbyes to Jhika Gali, the pleasant village just two miles uphill from camp.

Tuesday 9th. Our day of departure from Lower Topa. We have heard there has been trouble at Rawalpindi on our route but could not find out what sort of trouble. The journey has not been cancelled, so it must finally be safe to proceed.

The usual exciting journey by gharrie through the hills, up and down (mostly down) to Rawalpindi, where we found guards on the train. There was no trouble that we could see.

Wednesday 10th. Passed through Lahore. There was no time to revisit all the familiar places. But in my mind's eye, I pictured the highlights of the region where I spent the first fifteen months of my stay in India. In my imagination, I travelled along the marvellous Mall, past the Revnell Services Club, Nedou's and Faletti's hotels, Government House, Lawrence Gardens with its Montgomery Hall, the office of the local newspaper, *The Civil & Military Gazette*, the Punjab Assembly Hall fronted by the Victoria Memorial statue, the General Post Office, the railway station, the University of the Punjab, and last but not least, the Zamzama Gun. Away from the Mall, there are the alleyways of Anarkali Bazaar, and of course, the Shalimar Gardens.

Just over thirty miles to the next important city on our route, Amritsar, about eighteen miles past the Pakistani Punjab border into Indian Punjab. As the train was passing through Amritsar, I recalled a short trip I made more than a year before.

A flashback to a missed Golden opportunity.

June 1946. I was offered a brief interlude from camp life, to escort some supplies to a place not far away. It would only be within a day as the destination is just thirty miles each way and this place was called Amritsar. This is a Punjabi word meaning 'Lake of Holy Nectar'.

The delivery would be made by a special vehicle, an articulated lorry nicknamed a Queen Mary. It is called this because the vehicle's length is forty feet, or maybe sixty. I'm not sure, but I know it is very long. A monster of 38 tons. Among the equipment we will be carrying is, in RAF lingo, Acid Sulphuric (33C/340). Every single item has its own reference number in two parts. In this case, the first part (33C) is in the group for general paints and painting materials, i.e. acids, and the second number (340), is for the specific item, i.e. Sulphuric. This is why the description of goods in the RAF is reversed. Of all the thousands of items I handled, I don't know why this is the only reference number I can remember, a bit of useless information now to me. The sulphuric acid was carried in large containers with the unusual name of carboys, usually made of glass and protected by an outer wooden casing. Very dangerous cargo, but well protected. It was to be delivered to a Sikh who proved to be a very friendly fellow, and after sorting out the business side, we were talking in general and he offered to take us around the Golden Temple, the spiritual and cultural centre of the Sikh religion and the holiest Gurdwara (religious complex). It was completed in 1577 AD and receives more visitors than the Taj Mahal, unbelievable! The Temple is also known as the Harmandir Sahib or Harimandir Sahib, meaning 'abode of God'.

I was very willing to see it, in fact anxious to visit it. But my driver said unfortunately he had to get back with the vehicle, so we had to turn down the kind offer. The Sikh said, "Never mind, the offer is open for when you can manage it." Unfortunately, I had no other opportunity to return to Amritsar before I left India. I have always regretted not being able to take up his kind offer.

Thursday 11th. We passed though Delhi, where again I let my imagination take me back to all those amazing places, the Wavell Club, the Red Fort, Jama Masjid, Connaught Place, the Secretariat, Council House, the Rashtrapati Bhavan, along the Kingsway to the India Gate, two marvels of the ancient world Qutb Minar and Purana Qila, St. James Church and Kashmir Gate, both notable in the Indian Mutiny of 1857, and the Birla Mandir Temple. My mind wandered ahead of the train, south of Delhi to Agra, to the Red Fort and to the masterpiece of all masterpieces, the Taj Mahal.

Saturday 13th. Arrived at our camp at Allahabad, without encountering any trouble or rioting. I was told there was post waiting for me - a reply from Lotus? When I collected it, I opened it quickly. It was from the Mount View Hotel, but not from Lotus. It was from a new owner informing me that the previous owner and his family had left hastily without leaving a forwarding address. He added that he thought they were going to Delhi.

Had Lotus left Kashmir without letting me know where she was going with the family? Did it mean that she didn't want to continue with our romance? Did her father talk her out of it, with her being so young? So many questions! Dealing with that huge shock, it was about this time that I had orders for another escort duty. It would help to detract from the big problem of Lotus, but not very much.

This time the escort was for a much shorter journey than the previous one to Karachi. It was to a city called Jubbulpore a mere 200 miles each way, instead of the 758 miles each way for Karachi, also a much shorter stay, just overnight. Jubbulpore is now usually spelt Jabalpur. Unlike my other escort journeys, I cannot remember who or what I escorted. And with regard to sightseeing, I never managed any here and it seems that I missed out. The city appears to be picturesque, being surrounded by a series of lakes and numerous gorges.

Chapter 15
Departure Imminent

Sunday 14th Sept. Went into Allahabad and discovered an unusual 'shop'. It is called the India Coffee House. They were started around India in the early forties and after closing them down in the mid-fifties, the Coffee House chain recommenced opening them again and there are about four hundred at the present time in India now. The branch I went to in Allahabad served everything involving coffee, one of the most popular drinks in the world. It was discovered and consumed in Ethiopia as early as the ninth century. I found the iced coffee both cooling and refreshing in the heat of the day. They also served coffee ice cream, which I also tried. I thought it was very pleasant. I had never tasted it before and was surprised to realise that ice cream and coffee blended together so well. Something I never saw on the menu was coffee beans on toast, not that I would have ordered them if they were.

Monday 15th. Back on 'Work Parade' at 08.00 hours this morning, so it's a return to routine for the first time in over two months. And it isn't like in the heat of the summer, when we started earlier and finished by lunchtime. We now have to work later.

Tuesday 16th. Really feel back now, because the guard duty rota starts again tonight. It is my turn tomorrow night.

The India Coffee House.

Wednesday 17th. Reported this evening for my first guard duty at Allahabad, a night of patrolling the camp with a rifle. On my round, mostly uneventful, I suddenly started hearing a series of sounds. In the silence of the night, I heard them very loud and exaggerated. Was it a growl? No, more a low pitched, vibrating noise. I was contemplating if I should get my rifle ready. I didn't think it was a tiger. There are none in Allahabad, at least I didn't believe so. And anyway, it never sounded like the noise of a tiger. Whilst searching around in the darkness for any movement, I pondered on what kind of animal, or more to the point, what size of animal was making such a noise. At the very least, I expected a wild boar to charge out at any moment. After a few minutes, it became more peaceful, with no more repeats of the sound. Panic over. Returning to the Guard Room at the end of my shift, I asked what kind of animal it could have been and was informed that it was a bullfrog! I was told they can grow to six inches in length, a giant for a frog, but hardly the large wild animal that I had expected to leap out at me.

Saturday 20th. Went into town again and bought a pair of shoes, suede shoes. I thought I had got a bargain at about £1, but back in England with the first encounter of English rain, the suede started peeling off and it was too far to return them to the shop!

I also got weighed, very helpful. My weight, it read, was one maund and twenty-five seers. A maund unit is a weight in South Asia and varies from place to place but is often equal to 82 English pounds or 37 kilograms. I found out that a seer equalled 1/40 of a maund but varied considerably from one area to another. So, I never found out how much I weighed, as it was too complicated and unreliable to work out. However, I did get constructive help from the weight card, because on the reverse there was a printed proverb. And quoted in English, was the ingenious saying: "Blaze your own trail. Footsteps in the sands of time are not made by sitting down."

Monday 22nd. The Orders that we have been expecting so long have finally appeared. We are flying to Karachi on Wednesday with a rumour (only a rumour!) that we are being posted to Bulawayo in Southern Rhodesia. But the reality turned out to be that Karachi was the first stage of our journey back home to Blighty.

Tuesday 23rd. On my last day, I decided to attempt an 'expedition', actually a walk to the River Ganges near our camp. Ken and a couple of other lads accompanied me. I don't remember how we knew which direction to go, or even how far it was. It should have been easy to find because it is not a small river. We did locate it. It must have been a mile wide, even though it still had five hundred miles to travel before reaching the Bay of Bengal near Calcutta (Kolkata) and ultimately the Indian Ocean. A vast area of the Ganges Delta is extremely prone to floods in the monsoon season. On reaching the banks of the mighty Ganges, by now in the heat of the day, we had developed a thirst. We came across some kind villagers who took pity on us and offered us water. We took a gamble and accepted. Luckily, we had no after-effects with our European digestion. At the village, we also purchased a watermelon. One of our party had a penknife, which came in useful to share out the fruit. It quenched our thirst splendidly. On our return journey, we came across a tribe or mission of monkeys in some trees near our route. They didn't take as much notice of us, as we did of them. Probably they were too busy grooming themselves and also pestering each other.

A quiet harbour on the Ganges.

Sacred temple on the bank of the River Ganges.

A quiet corner of the village.

Drinking water, local style.

Wednesday 24th. Today is our real start to our journey back to Blighty. I believe the military had decided not to convey us by rail, because that would mean travelling about a thousand miles across territory still suffering from unrest and possibly violence, even though there has been a gradual decrease since Partition. Also, it would mean crossing the border from India to Pakistan, very difficult and perilous. Consequently, we are flying the eight hundred miles from RAF Bamrauli to Karachi in an Avro York. It has been recently converted from the Avro Lancaster Bomber, so notable in the bombing raids on Germany in the latter part of the Second World War. They are now masquerading as troop transporters and intended to be used in the future as a civilian passenger aircraft. If so, it would be the largest passenger carrier to date, with a wingspan of 102 feet, a length of 78 feet 6 inches and a height of 16 feet 6 inches. The wings, tail and undercarriage match the Lancaster. It would be able to carry fifty passengers a range of 1250 miles. Later on, there were plans for larger civil aircraft, such as the well-known and ill-fated Brabazon and the less famous Tudor.

Bamrauli was the location in the Indian sub-continent for the first flight of a 'heavier than air' aircraft, a Bleriot. It was piloted by an Englishman and the date was 10th December 1910! After the departure of the RAF, Bamrauli was also the place where the Indian Air Force established a pilot training establishment.

It was intended that the Avro York would, of course, be fitted out with seats for service as a civilian airliner. But for our transfer across the sub-continent, we didn't have such a 'luxury' as seats. We were sitting on the floor, leaning against the fuselage on both sides on the aircraft. Not very comfortable. Nevertheless, we arrived safely at our destination, Karachi.

Leaving camp at the start of our long journey home.

Thursday 25th. I made a return visit to Manora Island to refresh my memory of it.

Saturday 4th October. Today was the turn of Hawkes Bay to say goodbye.

Sunday 5th. For our last outing, Ken and I chose to do something completely different to anything else that we have done whilst in South Asia. We went on a fishing trip at Sandspit in Karachi Bay, by hiring a small fishing craft and, of course, the crew. Ken was much more 'at home' with the sea, being from the Portsmouth area, whereas it was my very first experience. I have no idea what kind of fish we were after. However, the only one we ever caught, we were informed by our native crew of one, was a blowfish. A very strange fish indeed, from the family called Tetraodontidae, which also included puffers, balloonfish, bubblefish, globefish, swellfish, toadfish and toadies, many highly toxic to humans. Even then, they are regarded as a delicacy in various parts of the world. The one we hooked was definitely a blowfish, because it started blowing itself up. Our fisherman friend threw it back into the sea, saying, "We don't keep them." I hoped it could deflate itself when it got back into the water where it belonged.

Tuesday 7th. I am very unclear as to where we were stationed in Karachi, whilst awaiting our ship. I believe it to be RAF Mauripur but cannot be sure. Wherever it was, the orders finally came through to state that we were to be ready to embark in the morning of the 9th. Our ship was to be the British India Steam Navigation Company vessel, MV Dunera, a reasonable size of 11,162 tons, 516 feet long and 63 feet in breadth. It had quite a history, and I'm sure many ex-servicemen and women will be familiar with the ship.

It was launched in Glasgow in May 1937. Up to the Second World War, it combined its service between troop carrier and a school cruising programme. During the war, one of the most notorious events in British maritime history was when it became refugee transport in July 1940 and conveyed 'enemy aliens', all males, from Liverpool to Australia. On board, there were 2036 Jewish Germans and Austrians, (who were virulently anti-Nazi and had escaped certain persecution in Europe) plus 506 German and Italian prisoners of war. The ship's capacity was to be only 1500, including crew, so it was a bit overcrowded for the long journey to Australia. Also, on the fifty-seven-day journey, there was the constant risk of enemy attack. By the time they reached Australia, the conditions were appalling on board. The Officer-in-Charge was court marshalled. All the passengers were interned behind barbed wire, but subsequently the authorities realised they had made a mistake. The Jewish refugees became 'friendly aliens' and were offered asylum. About half of them stayed on, the others had left for commitments elsewhere. The story became a famous television movie in 1985, with the title *The Dunera Boys.*

Among other notable services involving the Dunera, the vessel took part in the Sicily landings in 1943 and transported Allied troops to occupy Japan in 1945. The duty of troop carrier continued until 1960, when it entered service after a refit as an educational cruise ship, with 187 cabin passengers and 834 children in dormitories. The ship, after forty years of travelling the world over, was retired in 1967 and was then scrapped.

So, I would be joining a huge chunk of history on Thursday for twenty-two days on the 'cruise' between Karachi and Southampton. A distance of 5900 miles from port to port and each mile will take me further away from my darling Lotus. But it seems she has abandoned me.

MV Dunera.

Chapter 16
Back to Blighty, s-l-o-w-l-y

Thursday 9th October. As I boarded a gharrie, I realised this is my last trip in South Asia. I had mixed feelings. I was sad to be leaving, but now that the journey has started, I would like to be back home in England.

It brought to mind a song very popular in the First World War, to be precise, in 1916. It was composed by three men, namely A J Mills, F Godfrey and B Scott. The names were new to me. It was a long song, and the chorus started like this:

> *Take me back to dear old Blighty*
> *Put me on the train for London town*
> *Take me over there, drop me anywhere*
> *Liverpool, Leeds or Birmingham I don't care.*

I looked at my berthing (boarding) card and at the details: Draft no. 4056, Serial no. 674, Troopdeck E6, Mess table 146 and Berth 14. We embarked on the Dunera at 12.45 hours and finally started pulling away at 17.45 hours from the quayside at Keamari Docks, with a line of low one-storey buildings lining the background. I stayed on deck as the island of Manora with its distinctive and familiar lighthouse glided past on our starboard side.

The vessel eased its way out of the bay into the spacious Arabian Sea. I turned to look back at the land and watched the sub-continent disappearing from sight over the horizon. And for every mile I travelled, I moved another mile further away from Lotus.

Convoy to the ship.

The Dunera awaits her passengers.

Another famous troopship, the Empire Windrush, hiding behind a dhow.

The last sight of Manora Island and its lighthouse. Also the final glimpse of the huge sub-continent.

An unexpected thought occurred to me. Twenty months ago, when I arrived by air, I landed in Karachi, INDIA. Here I am now leaving by sea from Karachi, PAKISTAN. Now, it is full steam ahead to Blighty, except for a couple of stops at ports in all the 5900 miles.

Going down below to my sleeping quarters, I discovered something unexpected. In true traditional sailor style, on the voyage we were sleeping in hammocks. Not only that, but we had to take them off the hooks every morning, to provide us with more room during the day. I found it a bit of a hassle at first. It soon became a routine and no problem. Also, I surprisingly found the hammock quite comfortable and never fell out once!

Friday 10th. At noon every day, over the ship's tannoy system would be announced the total mileage the ship has travelled in the previous twenty-four hours. There would be a sweepstake run and the nearest would win or share the jackpot. On the normal day's travel, the ship covered between 294 to 324 miles. Needless to say, I never got close with the correct mileage.

Saturday 11th. By now, we are well into the Arabian Sea. Not the biggest sea in the world. Nevertheless, still about 1200 miles across from Karachi to the African coast at Somalia. And at a maximum depth of 15,000 feet, that constitutes a lot of water. A lot of the lads were taking advantage of the 'cruise' on B deck, sunbathing in the low eighties Fahrenheit temperature.

Relaxing on B Deck aft.

Sunday 12th. Over the tannoy, there were also regular broadcasts of music. Oddly enough, only one piece of music made a big impression on me at the time and is the only one that I could remember. It is still a favourite of mine after all these years. It is a classical piece, to be precise it is a symphonic suite and was composed by Nicolai Rimsky-Korsakov, about sixty years previously. The title is *Scheherazade* and considered to be one of his most popular works. Parts of it were adapted in a ballet scene that closes a motion picture called *Song of Scheherazade*, in which the lead actress, Yvonne de Carlo, was also the principal dancer. On our voyage, it was most appropriate to be played for two distinct reasons. First, it is based on the tale of the *Thousand and One Arabian Nights*. In this narrative, Scheherazade persuades King (Sultan) Shahryar to stop his practice of marrying and executing a new bride daily. Such misogyny had motivated the King, after the discovery of his original wife's infidelity. Scheherazade survives by commencing a fascinating tale for the King every evening, leaving each unfinished and promising to complete it the following evening. She thus keeps him in suspense and prolongs her life from day to day. It is on the thousand and first night of their married life that she, having borne the King three male children, finally induces him to abandon his intention of executing her. With the music of these tales of the Arabian Nights, it is fitting to listen to it, during the crossing of the Arabian Sea.

The second reason is that the orchestral work portrays an image of the sea perfectly, in all its surging and tranquil moods. During his career as a sailor, Rimsky-Korsakov made a voyage of two and a half years between 1862 and 1865 but seems to have never sailed further than the Mediterranean. Even so, it was the influence of this earlier vocation that persuaded him to include the sea in the first and final movement of his composition. At first more calmly, then in the finale the sea breaks through noisily and works up to a climactic shipwreck on the rocks. For me on board, there were some rough moments, but nothing as dramatic as that, fortunately.

Ken and I had plenty of time to chat about things in general, but an important part was about our futures.

"When I get home a priority is to discuss with Penny the dates we are to get engaged and married. I think we could be engaged before I report to our new camp in England and wait until I am demobbed to get married. But of course, I have to find out what she thinks. It will be a joint decision. But whenever it is, I'm hoping you will be able to join us for both events."

"Yes, I will certainly do my best to share it with you both and it will definitely have to be a joint decision," I paused, deep in thought. "All the talk about engagements and weddings brings to my mind about Lotus. I am continually thinking about her. I can't understand why I haven't heard. I can't get her out of my mind. She has suddenly stopped writing. Is she safe with all the horrific things happening connected to Partition? Did she think the five days was just a holiday romance? Has she changed her mind? Is she…?"

"Regarding that," Ken interrupted, "When we were leaving Srinagar, Lotus really did appear to be genuinely upset. What I saw was a natural reaction and not an act."

"I give you that, but she left Srinagar without letting me know, there is just no answer to that." I was left deep in thought. All this time we were moving further and further away from her. My beloved Lotus.

Aden, barely appearing out of the sea mist.

Steamer Point, Aden.

Tuesday 14th. On our fourth day out of Karachi, we had crossed the Arabian Sea and had entered the Gulf of Aden. I believe it was peaceful then, but in the early part of the twenty-first century, it became known as 'Pirate Alley' owing to the amount of pirate activity in the area. Near the other end of this gulf, we reach, obviously, the British Crown Colony of Aden.

Aden, an important anchorage en route to the East. I cannot be sure, but I believe that our ship and possibly all the larger ones at the time, anchored off Steamer Point (now known as Tawahi). We were transferred ashore by motor launch. I didn't go anywhere specific whilst in Aden. I do, however, recall a meal I had there. It was curried chicken. Remarkably, I had just spent the best part of two years in India and had never sampled it there, in all that time. But it has been a favourite food of mine ever since.

Wednesday 15th. We sailed away from Aden after a twenty-hour stopover and soon (after about a hundred miles!) turned into a northerly direction through the gateway to the Red Sea. The real name of this narrow waterway is the Bab el Mandeb, it has been branded the 'Gate of Tears'. Although it is only twenty miles or so across (Africa to port, Asia to starboard), it is noted for the dangers of navigation in its waters. Another theory for its nickname, according to legend there was a powerful earthquake with the loss of many lives, so violent that it split Asia from Africa. From the Gulf of Aden, through the Bab el Mandeb Strait and into the Red Sea, the countries on the African side are collectively known as the Horn of Africa. They consist of Somalia, Ethiopia, Djibouti and Eritrea. The area certainly has immense problems. It is one of the most complex and disputed regions of the world, culminating in being a major source of terrorism. It is also reputed to be the hottest place on earth, particularly the Danakil Desert, homeland of the Afar people.

Thursday 16th. Into the Red Sea. We have to pass through the full length, all 1200 miles of it. It is 220 miles wide in places and a maximum depth of 7000 feet. The Red Sea has extensive shallow shelves, noted for marine life and corals, making it the world's most northerly tropical sea. That gives the impression that it would be serene and peaceful. Not to be! The ship is rolling quite a bit. Anyone who has been on a voyage on the sea or ocean will know that the rolling from side to side for some reason makes a person more prone to seasickness, than the motion of bow to stern. With that movement, waves attacking the ship from the front, the bow sometimes disappears into the upsurge and we hope it will emerge again. It is enough to put you off. However, I still enjoy sailing in all conditions.

Friday 17th. This was the day we broke the record of the most miles travelled in a twenty-four-hour period, 324, a fraction under fourteen miles an hour.

Saturday 18th. We dock at Port Sudan, founded by, yes, the British in 1909. After the record mileage yesterday, this time due to our stop here, our mileage was very low at only 172 miles. I was allowed shore leave. The only thing that I can recall about it, was that I managed to find my way to a beach. I don't know how or where. I remember it was a pebbly beach and being on the continent (Africa) which is well-known for animals, I expected at any minute for a wild 'something' to launch an attack! However, the outing was uneventful, but at least we stretched our legs on dry land for a while.

After leaving Port Sudan, we discovered that there would be no more shore leave. There were two up to now and despite the fact that we had travelled less than a third of the way, there would be no more. And we still had 4005 miles left to reach Blighty. A long time on board without a break.

Monday 20th. We entered the Gulf of Suez and at 07.00 the ship anchored at Port Tewfik. It is at the entrance to the Suez Canal, opposite the seaport town of Suez (in Egyptian as 'Suways'), no doubt to await authorisation to enter the Canal.

This is important for an array of sea traffic at Port Sudan. Control, because mostly it is one way, with the main passing places at the lakes, Little Bitter Lake, Great Bitter Lake and Lake Timsah.

Remarkably, in all its hundred miles plus, it has no locks. The two seas to which it connects, Red and Mediterranean, are virtually on the same level. We ultimately entered the Suez Canal at 17.50 after a long wait of over ten hours and arrived at the Bitter Lakes in the late evening. Thus, we travelled through during the night. Not that I would have known, but the average transit time normally takes around fifteen hours. The Canal was supervised and constructed by a French engineer, Ferdinand De Lesseps and opened in 1869. The history surrounding it is so varied. I will leave that for the history books to deal with. However, I must say who officially opened it. It was Empress Eugenie of France, the wife of Napoleon III. What I thought was extraordinary was her name. She was born Dona Maria Eugenia Ignacia Agustina de Palafox de Guzman Portocarrero y Kirkpatrick, 16th Marchioness of Ardales, 18th Marchioness of Moya, 19th Countess of Teba, 10th Countess of Montijo and ?th Countess of Ablitas.

Tuesday 21st. I woke up thinking that something is different. I couldn't hear the ship's engine functioning. Nor could I feel much movement. When I looked out of the porthole, I discovered the vessel was anchored off Port Said (Bur Sa-id) at the northern (Mediterranean) end of the Suez Canal.

We pulled out of Port Said into the Mediterranean Sea at 06.30 hours, firstly in a northerly direction, then towards the west, with the full length of the Mediterranean Sea ahead of us, all 1815 miles of it! One of the last views of Port Said was the monument to De Lesseps, founder and builder of the Suez Canal in 1869.

An array of sea traffic at Port Sudan.

Port Said, through the porthole.

The De Lesseps Monument.

Now it was full steam ahead in the Mediterranean. This sea is almost completely enclosed by land. The Romans thought it the centre of their earth. They named it with the words medius (middle) and terra (earth/land). Its coastline comprises at least nine very popular sunshine countries, plus a few holiday islands as well.

Wednesday 22nd. Our second day in the Mediterranean and I expected it to be reasonably warm, even near the end of October. But we came into some very cold and rough weather. The tropical kit khaki uniforms started disappearing on deck, to be replaced by the more familiar thicker royal blue uniforms. I was on duty in the evening and the ship was pitching a bit, which continued during the night.

Thursday 23rd. To compensate for no shore leave, a concert was organised on board, also a cinema. All the service personnel were now wearing blue. It seems that the Suez Canal divides the hot weather from the cold, at least at the end of October.

Friday 24th. Passed between Malta and Sicily today. Malta itself is on the 'crossroads of the Mediterranean', a strategic position influencing its history throughout the centuries. Less than six years earlier, in April 1942, the island as a whole was awarded the George Cross by King George VI, to honour the courage of the inhabitants during the Second World War. A hundred miles further on, we could see the very small Italian island of Pantellaria, situated between Sicily and Tunisia, neither of which were visible from our ship as we passed.

Saturday 25th. Full steam ahead in a westerly direction, following the line of the North African continent, with the glimpses of the Tunisian coast appearing at intervals. Somewhere in the mist or haze was the most northerly and the nearest Tunisian city to our ship, Bizerte. It was just a bit too far to discern. Nonetheless, it sounds an interesting place. Occupied until 1963 by France, it is the most French and European city in

Africa and the oldest city in Tunisia, being founded by the Phoenicians in 1000BC. The double Kasbah is a mere four hundred years old! The buildings at the port are in the beautiful colours of greyish white and pale blue. But the sight was not visible to us on board.

Monday 27th. Sunrise. The coast of southern Spain emerges on our starboard side, from about five miles out at sea. The red sunshine from the southeast and the Sierra Nevada range of mountains combined to create a great picture, a pity just too far away to take a photograph.

At 16.30, we were passing the famous and familiar landmark of Gibraltar, which was unfortunately shrouded in cloud, but still identifiable. There is such an enormous amount of history connected to the 'Rock', owing to its strategic position guarding the entrance to the Mediterranean Sea from the Atlantic Ocean. The name Gibraltar is derived from the Arabic for Jabal Tariq, 'the mountain of Tariq'. He was Tariq ibn Ziyad, a Berber General who invaded the Iberian Peninsula in the year AD711. Gibraltar has been British territory since AD1704 and legend claims it will remain with Britain while the renowned and mischievous Barbary apes exist there. Also, it has been said that the Gibraltarians are more British than the British! Many, many years after this day of passing Gibraltar without stopping, I spent an enjoyable long weekend on the Rock and remember visiting a very pleasant little restaurant at Catalan Bay and having a meal of swordfish, also very pleasant. But making the most influence on me were two windows of this restaurant. One framed a scene of Europe, the Costa del Sol in Spain, and the other surrounded a vista of Africa on the Moroccan shoreline. Two continents for the price of one!

The African coast is only eight or nine miles away across the Strait of Gibraltar, with a depth varying between 1000 to 3000 feet. The town Ceuta in Morocco is almost opposite Gibraltar and is considered part of Spain (Andalucia). There is a direct ferry to Tangier, which is a city about thirty miles further west along the Moroccan coast, in fact not in the Mediterranean, but in the mighty Atlantic.

Subsequently, when in Gibraltar for the long weekend, I sampled this ferry service and spent a day in Tangier, wandering around the Casbah. I came across a snake charmer where, for a while, I borrowed his snake (not a King Cobra) to wear as a scarf. Contrary to belief, they are not cold blooded.

On the national news it was reported that yesterday, Sunday 26th October, Baramula was captured by invading tribal militia men. The invasion was called 'Operation Gulmarg' and the objective was to eventually take over occupation of Kashmir. The whole situation was highly complicated, even when attempting to explain it in simple terms. The attack actually commenced earlier in the month, with the city of Muzaffarabad taken a few days previously. The aim was to continue along the Vale of Kashmir and occupy Srinagar, its airport and Gulmarg. But the invasion stalled at Baramula (a mere thirty-three miles before Srinagar) for three days of looting, burning, abductions and rapes.

I was so anxious and worried. What has become of my beloved Lotus and her family?

To the North – Gibraltar in a blanket of low cloud.

Tuesday 28th. Before morning parade, we passed about three miles from Cape St. Vincent, the most south-westerly point of Europe and only about fifteen miles from the popular Portuguese resort of Lagos. At this Cape, the cliffs rise vertically for a height of 230 feet.

Just before dark, we reached Cabo da Roca, near Lisbon, and the most westerly point in mainland Europe. If there was time to visit this Cape, at the lighthouse there is an inscription: "Aqui – onde a terra se acaba e o mar comeca." When translated from the Portuguese it reads, "Here – where the land ends and the sea begins." The cliffs here are even higher than at Cape St. Vincent, rising at least 430 feet above sea level. In this area we saw many fishing smacks and squibs, the latter being a racing keelboat (similar to a yacht) no more than twenty feet long with a crew of two.

Wednesday 29th. Very cold today. It was getting dark when we passed Cape Finisterre with its prominent lighthouse. Heading in the direction of England, this is to indicate that the ship is shortly to be entering the notorious Bay of Biscay, the very name caused dread among the ancient mariners and the not so ancient. It is the natural home to some of the Atlantic's fiercest storms, particularly in the winter. What could be ahead of us? We had that obstacle between us and Blighty. Consequently, it was inevitable that we sailed into the Bay, into rather a rough and extremely cold night.

Thursday 30th. At about 21.00 hours we passed the Phare du Creac'h, a group of three lighthouses. The most important of the group is more recognisable as Ushant (d'Ouessant in French), an offshore lighthouse built at a height of almost 170 feet in 1863. This group is situated at the tip of the Breton (Brittany) peninsular and is twenty-five miles from the city of Brest, an important seaport and naval base. The city played a big part in the Second World War, because it was a large submarine base for the Germans during the battle of the Atlantic. It was totally destroyed in 1944, except for barely three buildings left standing. It is now twinned with Plymouth in England along with many others around the world. The main lighthouse of the group is reputed to being the most powerful in the world. It needs to be, because this northwest corner is prone to the most penetrating autumn and winter storms. Our ship has timed it just right, well into autumn! After passing Ushant, the ship set course in a north-easterly direction, almost immediately entering the English Channel and very close to our destination and home.

Friday 31st. My fears for the wild Bay of Biscay and around Ushant never materialised. The weather was reasonable and the ship didn't need to struggle through a storm or mountainous seas. Nearing the end of our voyage and reminiscing about it, I realise that I mentioned very little about life on board. After many days at sea, it does become routine. Particularly when there is no shore leave, of which we had none since Port Sudan, almost four thousand miles back on our route. The 'passing parade' of the world drifting by the ship was much more engrossing. Whichever way you looked, there was always something of interest, fascinating facts, amazing and amusing details. Great excitement on board at 15.00 hours. Our first sight of England, in my case for twenty-one months. To uncountable millions, it is the first view of England from wherever in the world. Being accurate, it is not the mainland. It was the Needles, cliffs on the Isle of Wight.

The very first object to reach is the lighthouse, not as tall as most at only one hundred feet above the sea. Following close behind, is a series of three distinctive masses of chalk rising from the water. None of them is shaped like a needle. But evidently, there used to be a fourth that resembled a needle. However, it collapsed into the sea in 1764 and the name remained over the centuries!

Not long after passing the Needles, the ship turns into Southampton Water. At 17.30, it ultimately docks at the Port of Southampton, a major port connected strongly with the Cunard Line. At the quay, there was a pleasant touch. An RAF band was playing to greet us back to Blighty, or could it possibly be because the liner Queen Mary was docked nearby!

The first glimpse of England---The Needles, Isle of Wight.

The Green and Pleasant Land — in black and white

Chapter 17
Back in Blighty

Saturday 1st November. We were issued with rations for our forthcoming journey by train and we finally disembarked at 03.30 hours. Ken was leaving on a different train, because his train would be travelling south to the Portsmouth area. I don't know when he left, but my troop train didn't leave until 10.15, with a destination unknown. We guessed it would be London, sixty miles away. We certainly headed in that direction, travelling through Basingstoke at 11.45. Now only 32 miles from London, a mere 'flea jump' after our journey from India. We passed Woking at 12.00, then Wimbledon, Clapham Junction and Kensington. Some of the words came back to me of the song, *Take me back to dear old Blighty*. That is the line, "Put me on the train for London Town." They finally did. No, they didn't. The train suddenly veered to the north and we found ourselves passing through Rugby, Stafford and Crewe. We eventually arrived at our destination, RAF Burtonwood, near Warrington in Lancashire, from where we would be dispersed to our various postings around Britain.

Sunday 2nd. We were less than twenty-four hours at camp and then on our way out for disembarkation leave I was back home in Birmingham at 22.00 hours.

Monday 3rd. My first full day back home after being twenty-one months overseas. Ma asked me to bring her up to date.

"Well, I was supplying equipment for various camps and going on sentry or fire duty. But what I enjoyed was sightseeing, chiefly in India and Pakistan. The two places that impressed me most were the Taj Mahal and Kashmir in the Himalayan Mountains. I was only in Kashmir for five days and was friendly with a girl of sixteen. I was told she is too young to be serious but she is only four years younger than me. When I went back to camp, we corresponded for nearly two months, then she stopped writing and we lost touch."

"Quite right." Ma remarked. "You are much too young to be serious, particularly with someone so far away."

I never took her comments any further, but it was so very hard for me to concentrate on other matters when I couldn't get Lotus out of my mind. However, life must go on. So, I forced myself whilst on leave to wonder where in Britain I will conclude my National Service. No doubt it would be just about as far away from my home in Birmingham as is possible, without going overseas. However, I underestimated the RAF. After my leave, I was posted to RAF 216 Maintenance Unit at Sutton Coldfield only eight miles from my home in Birmingham. And that in itself was a bit of a coincidence, because my main camp in India was also eight miles from Lahore, the nearest sizeable place. I was to report on 21st November to my new camp after my leave had finished.

Saturday 8th. Received a letter from Ken letting me know that he and Penny will be having an engagement party on Saturday 15th. I wrote back to let him know that I will come for the weekend and I'll book a hotel in his area.

Friday 14th. Travelled down to the Portsmouth area for the engagement party and was happy to see Ken again. We had been through a lot of adventures together. And, of course, I met Ken's fiancée Penny for the first time. All three of us got on well.

"Since Penny and I announced our engagement," he said, "all our friends now call us Ken and Pen. Inseparable."

"Yes. I can see you are made for each other. I'm certain you are assured a long and a happy life."

So many things remind me of Lotus and my mind wanders to the first three lines of 'The Kashmiri Song':

Pale hands I loved beside the Shalimar.
Where are you now?
Who lies beneath your spell?

Suddenly, I realised Ken was talking. "I know who you are thinking about!"

"There's just no hope for me," I said.

"No. You are wrong," commented Penny, "It will happen for you, probably when you least expect it."

"It's already happened to me, Penny. And I lost."

"Never give up hope. You have plenty of time, because you are still very young." she said.

Saturday 15th November. The engagement party went well down near Portsmouth and everyone enjoyed themselves, particularly Ken and Penny. They spoke about possibly arranging to be married when Ken is demobbed within the next few months.

Friday 21st November. I duly reported to RAF216 Maintenance Unit at Sutton Coldfield for my first assignment since arriving back from overseas service. Most ex-RAF personnel would be aware of the RAF form 252 Charge Report. It is used to record any misdemeanour, misconduct, misbehaviour or wrongdoing. The closest to being on one for the first and only time in my RAF career happened at Sutton Coldfield. It came about unexpectedly during my very first kit inspection. Although all my kit display conformed to regulations, one item let me down. I was displaying RAF shoes and not boots. The officer inspecting asked, "Where are your boots?" It was very tricky, until I explained that I had just returned from overseas and had never been issued with boots. The officer was satisfied with that, but I have been puzzled sometimes as to what I wore with my uniform for the few months, that is until I went to Heaton Park, Manchester, for the issue of my tropical kit. What did I wear on my feet all through my 'Square Bashing' and trade training? I'll never know!

Another time on kit inspection, when on his round the inspecting officer noticed some pin-ups (Betty Grable, etc.) on somebody's locker – not mine. He studied them for a short while then said, "Remove those lush thrushes." They were taken off for a while, then replaced later.

I obtained a 36-hour pass for several weekends before Christmas. One time on my return to camp, I was a bit late arriving at the bus station from home and actually saw my last bus, which passed the camp, leaving from the centre of Birmingham. It stopped at traffic lights. I rushed up to catch it but missed it there as well. I had to settle for a bus to Sutton Coldfield and had the eight-mile hike back to camp from there.

It wasn't long before I was assigned to fire picket duty, moving into the fire billet for a week, to enable me to carry out my duties. It sounds very impressive but turned out to be a very easy duty. I spent a lot of time in the NAAFI Canteen, listening to records being played there and in the billet itself, there was a 'wizard' radio. So, my duty consisted mainly of music, writing and a bit of reading. A lot better than most in the forces. It was just a matter of standing by on camp for the week in case there is a fire. But there was the serious side to Fire Picket Duty.

Saturday 13th December. I sent a letter to Ken telling them that I met a girl named Laura a short while ago and we are getting engaged on Sunday 21st December and hope that they can both come. They answered by return and said they would be delighted to attend. But Ken also wrote about a comment that Penny made when she read that I am to be engaged. She says that I have wasted no time in meeting someone and it was only a short month ago that she said it would happen eventually. But she never thought it would happen so quickly. And Penny wonders if you are rushing things too much.

Over the Christmas period, I couldn't avoid comparing this year with last year's experiences in India. There was no comparison really, except for one redeeming factor. RAF Sutton Coldfield presented a seasonal show. It was entitled 'A chance to dream' and some of the audience thought it was corny. Only an amateur production, but it turned out to be a very professional production. It featured a very new song, a fun song, 'Civilization', composed in 1947 by Bob Hilliard and Carl Sigman. It was recorded the same year by Danny Kaye with the Andrews Sisters (possibly the very first girl band!) The words are exceedingly clever, comparing the jungle favourably to civilisation in the city.

There was another song in the show that stayed in my mind. Very different to 'Civilization', this masterpiece was called 'Winter Wonderland', composed in 1934 and still very popular to the present day. The creators were Felix Bernard (music) and Richard B. Smith (lyrics). So many different artists recorded it over the years, such as Tony Bennett, Karen Carpenter, Perry Como, Bing Crosby, Rosemary Clooney, Eurythmics, Elvis Presley, Dean Martin, Johnny Mathis, Dolly Parton, and Frank Sinatra, to name but a few. Quite a collection. How many do you remember or have even heard of? The total number of artists recording it must be about one hundred and fifty! Surprisingly, the composition is regarded as a Christmas song in the northern hemisphere, even though the holiday is not mentioned specifically in the lyrics. But there is reference to sleigh bells occasionally.

Friday 19th. Ken and Penny arrived the day before our engagement. We were both on duty over Christmas, Ken at his camp near Portsmouth and me at Sutton Coldfield.

So, Laura and I decided to celebrate our day on the Saturday before. There were ten expected to come at teatime for our engagement, but Ken and Penny were arriving in time for lunch after their longish journey from the south coast.

When they arrived, Laura had gone just gone out shopping for a couple of items for the afternoon and while waiting for her, we were chatting.

"Are you on fire duty over Christmas, Ken?"

"Yes," he acknowledged, "We have to take our turn, I suppose."

"Me too," I agreed. I was just going to continue when we heard the front door open and close. "Ah. That will be Laura."

We stood up to greet her and Ken started to say, "It's good to meet you Lau…" and stopped in amazement and puzzlement, recovered quickly and continued, "You are not Laura. Could you really be Lotus?" It wasn't a question, just a statement of fact.

The girl giggled, then laughed. "Yes, you are quite right, Ken. It is me!"

"How do you come to be here?" Ken asked, very puzzled, and then he turned to me, "Why didn't you let me know in advance?"

"Because I wanted your reaction. It was also very unexpected for me too. I could never have imagined it in a thousand dreams!"

"How do you come to be here, Lotus?" Ken repeated.

I intercepted, "It's quite a long story. After lunch we will tell you."

Chapter 18
A New Beginning

After lunch we settled down to relate the events as they happened and it starts only a month ago when I reported at my new posting in England. I went through the usual procedures when arriving for the first time at a new camp. After all the formalities were completed, I turned away and I was called back.

"I have just seen a note against your name," I was told.

"What's the problem?"

"No problem. You have mail! I'll get it for you."

He came back after a couple of minutes or so. "No, there's not one letter. You're a popular lad. You have two "

After thanking him for them, I searched for my billet, found it, and settled down at my bedside to read them. I was mystified as to who would be sending them.

The first one was extremely interesting before I even opened it. It was addressed to me at Lower Topa and redirected to me via my camp at Allahabad. I had gone from there, so it followed me to the camp at RAF Mauripur, Karachi, in Pakistan. It then followed me all the way back to England and was finally delivered to Sutton Coldfield. It was dated the 8th of September, the day before I actually left the Hill Station. It took slightly over a total of ten weeks to reach me. Finally, with shaking hands, I opened the letter. It was headed at the top with an address in Delhi and the letter was from Lotus.

With a huge amount of relief, but still puzzled, I read:

"My Dearest Bob,
I have something important to tell you. There is big talk here in Srinagar about a forthcoming invasion of tribal militia men who intend to occupy the Vale of Kashmir sometime next

month.
This is not a good thing for Hindus and Dad said that we are leaving Kashmir for our safety. You will see our Delhi address at the top of this letter. You probably remember that is where my dad originally came from.
I still miss you very much. You went away and my heart has gone with you.
Please write very soon.
Ever yours, Lotus."

My first reaction to her letter was great relief to know that she and the family were safe. As I picked up the second letter, my next thought was that Delhi is still much too far away from her. This envelope was like the first, redirected to me from Lower Topa, all the way to my camp in England. It was dated 14th October and I was anxious as I opened it.

The first thing I noticed was that it was also from Lotus. But at the head of this letter there was an address, this time not in Delhi but in England. Leeds in Yorkshire to be precise. Just about a hundred miles away! "What's this?" I blurted out to myself in surprise, an automatic reaction.

"My Dearest Bob,
I still have not heard from you. I hope you receive this letter because I have some bad news. I am so very sad to say that my dad was caught up in a riot in Delhi recently and he died in the fighting. It was so ironic because we all moved to Delhi to be safe. We were, and still are, all so emotionally shocked. It was then my mum decided for us to come to England to join her sister here in Leeds. Please write. I need you more than ever now. I am frightened that I will not hear from you again. Your Laura… Lotus of course."

It is imperative that I must write to Lotus today. She has waited too long for replies. Luckily, there were no camp duties at this time, so I started immediately.

"My Darling Lotus.
I have only this instant received your letters from Delhi and from England and it is important to me that I write to you immediately. It was a huge shock to hear about your dad. He was a true and kindly man. He tried to put me right with our relationship.
I have no more leave due before I finish my time with the RAF, but I should manage to arrange a couple of 36-hour passes until then. I'll let you know the dates as soon as possible. It is now four months since I left you. I felt guilty and upset about leaving you and I missed you so much every single day. Be assured I will come to you at the very first opportunity.
Love you always, Bob."

Two days later, I received an answer.

"I am so relieved to hear you finally received my letters. I cannot believe you are actually coming. It seems such a long time ago when I watched your bus leaving me. I will meet you at the station. Cannot wait, guess I will have to.
With love and anticipation, Laura."

By now, I had arranged my 36-hour pass, so I answered her letter saying that I will be arriving at City Station on Saturday 5th December, due in at 4 pm.

Saturday 5th December. At 3.58 the train pulled into Leeds and with some trepidation I made my way to the exit. Suddenly, there she was, standing before me. Neither of us moved for moments, not believing we had found each other again. Then we were cuddling and kissing. I was overwhelmed. Lotus was laughing and almost crying at the same time. It was all so emotional. Eventually we separated, nevertheless still holding hands in case one of us suddenly disappeared. Neither of us could believe we were actually together again. Lotus, Laura – I will have to get used to her name change. I keep forgetting.

After our emotional meeting, we succeeded in arriving at their house in the district of Roundhay and met her mother and brother.

"Good to see you again, Mrs Sharmer. Do you miss your hotels?"

"Yes, I do. But I intend to look for one here when we are more settled." She added, "My sister sends her apologies for not seeing you this weekend. She and the family are away this weekend. They would be pleased to meet you next time you are here."

I turned to Anand. "Hello young man. You seem to have grown since I saw you four months ago," I thought that was a silly thing to say, so I added "But I think you have." He had grown taller in that short time.

After we had lunch, Lotus said to me, "There is something I must show you this afternoon. I was very pleased to find it. It is in walking distance!"

With that, we set off walking hand in hand for a few minutes along a main road.

"Down at the bottom of the hill on the left is the entrance of one of Britain's largest city parks with the name of Roundhay," said Lotus, in her best travel guide voice.

"Ah! I notice you would still like to be a guide in England."

"Oh yes, but what I want to show you is on the right."

We continued down the road and very quickly we reached a doorway. We entered through a high wall and the scene that greeted me was unexpected. In front of me was the very end of a long waterway.

"This part is known as Canal Gardens. It was laid out as far back as 1833 and the waterway is 350 feet long from this spot and 34 feet wide. Spaced along the length are working jet fountains."

As I'm studying the scene, she asked, "Does it remind you of something?"

"Yes," I said. "It reminds me of the waterway at Shalimar Gardens, except for a couple of differences. Here at one end is just a small shelter for rain instead of the large Pavilion at Shalimar, where we first met. And at the other end, there are the tall trees instead of the mighty Himalayas. But I can see a resemblance with the waterway."

There are footpaths all around the waterway and we chose the left. No, Lotus chose the left and I followed. I noticed there were many seats along the path to sit and study the scene. About halfway, Lotus asked, "Shall we sit a while?"

I nodded and we sat down. It was unbelievable. My arm was around her shoulder and her arm was around my waist. I couldn't believe that this was really happening. Meeting after four months seems like a lifetime. Am I dreaming? Am I really with Lotus when I thought we were lost from each other forever? We sat like that for a while, then I stood up.

"What are you doing?" she asked. "Relax. Please sit down and cuddle me. I miss you!"

"I can't relax, there is something I have planned to do today," and I reached into my pocket, took out a small package and stood in front of her, then went down on one knee. I opened the box and Lotus looked down at a ring, a cornflower blue sapphire ring.

"Lotus, will you please marry me?"

I was studying the fountains whilst holding my breath.

Canal Gardens - Roundhay Park, Leeds.

In Canal Gardens, with 'our' seat, left of the fountains.

She was silent and seemed hypnotised, then she said, "Yes. Yes. Of course, I will."

As I was rising from the hard path, I groaned and declared, "That was a bit hard on my knee, but well worth it!"

While we were kissing, a couple was passing. They had obviously heard and seen it all. They stopped with a smile on their faces and both said, "Congratulations, have a good life." We thanked them and they continued their walk.

Meanwhile, Lotus asked breathlessly, "Can I wear it now?"

"I don't see why not, unless it doesn't fit properly."

I took it out of the box and placed it on her correct finger. She knew which one and it fitted perfectly. A true match. Ring and person. By now, she had recovered partially from her surprise and managed to ask, "Did you know that the cornflower blue sapphire is the gemstone of Kashmir?"

"Of course I did. That's why I chose it. I had over a week to research before I came here to Leeds. But I have to apologise. I wanted to get a genuine Kashmiri gemstone, but I discovered that the mining of them finished in the Himalayas earlier this century. So, they became exceedingly rare and impossibly expensive."

"Oh no. You do not have to apologise at all. It is so beautiful."

Without hesitation I replied, "Just like you."

We just relaxed cuddling in the seat for a while, until Lotus enlightened me. "Opposite here on the other side of the waterway, there is an entrance through to the Vegetable Garden. It was established in 1816. It is also known as the Coronation Garden and later as the Rose Garden." Lotus told me it was on the way home from here, so after relaxing and cuddling for a short while longer, we walked slowly through the garden adjoining Canal Gardens and discovered that the garden was now laid out with fewer vegetable patches and with more rose bushes and herbaceous plants.

When Lotus and I arrived back at her home, I sensed the feeling that her mum appeared to have mixed feelings about me, but after an intrigued look at the ring she said to us, "It's a perfect ring. Congratulations to you both. I am very pleased for the two of you. But you knew your dad's thoughts about it, thinking you were too young at sixteen. Bob, did you know that it was mostly Lotus who wanted to move to Britain more than I did. When she received no replies from you to her letters, she was very upset. She wanted to come and try to find you here in England!"

"No, I never realised that. I just thought Lotus didn't want to continue with our friendship. All I knew was being extremely upset I never heard from her. However, the last letters she wrote were greatly delayed because I had left Lower Topa to return to my main camp and I didn't receive them until I reported to my camp here in England four months later. I now realise it was a huge mistake on my part not to give her my Allahabad address as well. I sent it too late, because Lotus had already left Srinagar and Kashmir to an address unknown. However, I have loved her since the very first day I saw her. I have thought of her every day since. I just thought Lotus didn't want to continue with our friendship."

A short time later, we enjoyed a meal, after which Lotus said, "I have not danced at all since we enjoyed dancing at the lounges at our hotels in Kashmir. Should we go to a dance in a real ballroom this evening?"

I replied, "It sounds an excellent idea. Let's do it. I haven't danced since then. I have been waiting to dance with you again."

"There is a ballroom not very far from here called the Astoria, down Roundhay Road. It was originally known as the Harehills Palais-de-Danse. I will go up to get ready. You will not need to, because the suit you are wearing will be fine." I was wearing my blue suit with a tie and white shirt. It was quite acceptable for the Dance Hall.

Lotus came back in and my immediate reaction was "Wow." She was wearing her red dress. "You look gorgeous." It brought back all the amazing memories of our unforgettable day at the lakes around Srinagar, our last full day together.

Her mum also approved and seemed pleased. "Off you go. Have a good time."

Lotus was right, it didn't take long before we reached the ballroom. Outside, the billboards announced:

Smartest Dancing and Dancing to two Star Bands.
Tues and Fri   7.30 to 11.00   One shilling & sixpence
Wednesdays   7.30 to 11.00   Two shillings & sixpence
Saturdays   7.30 to 11.30   Three shillings.
Also Drives available.

Current prices respectively are seven and a half pence, twelve and a half pence and fifteen pence. Drives? Whist Drives, of course. But we were only interested in the dancing. Not long after, it cost all of three shillings (15p) per ticket and we were inside the Astoria, shown to a table where we ordered drinks, not alcohol, just soft drinks for Lotus. I joined her with a soft drink. We were on the dance floor very soon after. The first dance was the song of the day called 'Near You', the music was written by Francis Craig and the lyrics by Kermit Goell. How appropriate the words were. I hoped that Lotus thought the same. With the words running through my mind, it was sublime to be dancing close to Lotus again, when I thought for months that I would never see her again and she would be lost forever. We stayed dancing to the very end, 11.30. The band always played half an hour longer on Saturdays.

Sunday 6th December. My train back to camp is due to leave at six o'clock. "I have to report to camp by…" I began.

With a little giggle, Lotus finished what I was going to say.

"By 23.59 hours. I remember too well!"

"We are not likely to ever forget the morning when I left you at Srinagar," I said, then added, "Yes, I know. Should we just take it easy today?"

"Yes. I would like that."

"Leaving you this evening will be difficult, Lotus, but at least we know we will meet again soon and regularly."

And we did constantly, until it was time for me to be demobbed.

1st March 1948. I have heard that I am to be demobbed on the 15th, so I have a mere two weeks' more service and I will be once again a member of the public, a much wiser one possibly. Hopefully in my time in the RAF, I have converted from a sprog to a seasoned airman and a respectable citizen.

15th March. I reported to the largest wartime air base in Europe. Known as RAF Burtonwood, it is situated two miles northeast of Warrington, about halfway between Liverpool and Manchester. During the war, it was said to be out of the range of enemy bombers, but in fact was raided several times. By the end of the war, 18,000 service personnel were stationed there. In the late fifties, the idea was put forward that the site would be ideal for a civil airport to service the two cities, but subsidence from coal mining in the area put paid to that idea.

There were two aspects of demobilisation, payment and leave. In a way, both are connected, in view of the paid demob leave. Added to my demob leave, like all others at this time, I received one day for every month served overseas. After demob, in my case this totalled to a considerable amount, in fact eleven weeks. I went back to work before the demob leave finished. There was a regulation that your employer had to re-employ you after serving in the forces, and for me, that worked out OK. So, it was back to work as a cinema projectionist and I enjoyed it, except it involved unconventional hours. I still had in my mind to open my own travel agency in the future.

One of the final acts before I finished completely, was that all ex-servicemen were presented with a demob suit. To this day, I ponder on why on earth I picked a *brown* suit. I never liked it. Or perhaps I got more accustomed than I thought to the blue uniform of the RAF.

Pondering on my experiences in the RAF, I have created my favorite 3-2-1, not related to the old game show on television many years ago with Ted Rogers. Number three would be the amazing Christmas at 306MU Lahore, next would be the stunning Taj Mahal, and the crowning glory would be Kashmir. A country with great misfortune, that has been the hub of a lethal dispute for decades. It is the world's oldest unsolved dispute. A region so unique, it needs essentially to be an entity on its own, with the help of outside assistance.

In the course of my being away from the Blighty shores with the Royal Air Force, I have experienced and travelled on a diverse range of transport. Ships, planes, trains, buses, lorries, bicycles, tongas, ambulances, ferries, bunder boats, a dukw and last but certainly not least, the shikara. Additionally, it is surprising how the mileages add up – 5900 miles by sea, also 5900 by air (including the flight across the sub-continent), an impressive 5867 miles by train, and a meagre 520 all in Kashmir by bus – but what a bus!

Reflecting on my Service career and taking everything into account, I enjoyed my National Service. Even when an individual with two or three stripes on his shoulder yelled at you and you just had to take it, without being able or expected to retaliate. If that is not understandable, then ask any ex-serviceman or woman to explain! It did me no harm and in fact, it taught me self-reliance, working as a team, pride, humility and introduced me to the marvellous world and how to appreciate it. Having experienced it at first-hand, perhaps National Service or conscription could be the answer to problems prevalent in the twenty-first century. And it would give a good foundation for responsible behaviour for future generations of anti-social behaviour, vandalism and delinquency.

Whilst in South Asia, I had in mind to visit many destinations. Some I achieved, like Kashmir, Delhi and Agra. But many more were missed. Objectives were Bombay and Calcutta, Darjeeling (I experienced Lower Topa instead), Ceylon (now called Sri Lanka) and Southern India (namely Kerala, Madras, Bangalore and Cochin). Looking at my list, I have realised that in the course of time the majority of the place names have been altered, probably because of the influence of Partition.

It was an honour to have served in the RAF. I have often thought that if I were six years older, I could have ended up in any part of the world involved in the Second World War and in any situation. When call-up came, I never gave it a thought and simply followed events. I am sure that youth, if called upon, would rally in any era. All would follow in any circumstance. I found that the good outweighed the not so good.

After completing my demob, my first priority was to visit Lotus and for us to journey together back to Canal Gardens. Something we accomplished very quickly. Sitting on 'our' seat facing the fountains, we were contemplating our romance. We agreed that Kismet triumphed. It was our destiny to be together.

"We so nearly lost each other," Lotus recalled, "after that astonishing five days."

"Yes indeed," I agreed, "Five minutes, five days or five years. It makes no difference, because scientists have said there is such a thing as love at first sight. And I have proved it. As soon as you turned round to me when we first met, I knew, even though I was lecturing you at the time. However, it was a marvel it didn't put you off."

"I must say it did, but for a very short time," Lotus admitted,

"Even before I left Shalimar, I forgave you."

"Now we can look forward to our marriage. A new beginning. I must mention that to honour your dad's wishes, we should not marry until you are at least turned eighteen."

"I completely agree and I am very happy that you mentioned it first."

"Perhaps at the start of the next decade, the fifties, during which you will reach nineteen, we can marry," I said, and predicted with a smile, "maybe then, we will have a Lotus of our own," to which Lotus added with a giggle, "or maybe two!"